REVIEWS OF OTHER BOOKS BY SEAN GABB

"Fascinating to read, very well written, an intriguing plot and I enjoyed it very much."
(Derek Jacobi, star of *I Claudius* and *Gladiator*)

"Vivid characters, devious plotting and buckets of gore are enhanced by his unfamiliar choice of period. Nasty, fun and educational."
(*The Daily Telegraph*)

"He knows how to deliver a fast-paced story and his grasp of the period is impressively detailed."
(*The Mail on Sunday*)

"A rollicking and raunchy read . . . Anyone who enjoys their history with large dollops of action, sex, intrigue and, above all, fun will absolutely love this novel."
(*Historical Novels*)

"As always, [his] plotting is as brilliantly devious as the mind of his sardonic and very earthy hero. This is a story of villainy that reels you in from its prosaic opening through a series of death-defying thrills and spills."
(*The Lancashire Evening Post*)

"It would be hard to over-praise this extraordinary series, a near-perfect blend of historical detail and atmosphere with the plot of a conspiracy thriller, vivid characters, high philosophy and vulgar comedy."
(*The Morning Star*)

OTHER BOOKS BY SEAN GABB

Acts of the Apostles: A Parallel Text
Aeneid XI with Notes and Vocabulary
Ars Grammatica
The Churchill Memorandum
The Column of Phocas
Cultural Revolution, Culture War
Dispatches from a Dying Country
Literary Essays
Radical Coup
Return of the Skolli
Smoking, Class and the Legitimation of Power
Stories from the Life of Christ
Stories from Paul the Lombard
War and the National Interest
The York Deviation

WRITING AS RICHARD BLAKE

Writing as Richard Blake
Conspiracies of Rome
Terror of Constantinople
Blood of Alexandria
Sword of Damascus
Ghosts of Athens
Curse of Babylon
Game of Empires
Death in Ravenna
Crown of Empire
Death of Rome I
Death of Rome II
The Devil's Treasure
The Boy from Aquileia
The Tyburn Guinea
The Break
How I Write Historical Fiction

Sean Gabb is a writer and teacher whose books have been translated into German, Italian, Spanish, Greek, Hungarian, Slovak and Chinese. He also directs the Centre for Ancient Studies.
He lives in Kent with his wife and daughter

FREEDOM OF SPEECH IN ENGLAND:

ITS PRESENT STATE AND LIKELY PROSPECTS

TWENTY ESSAYS WITH
AN INTRODUCTORY OVERVIEW

BY SEAN GABB

"Give me the liberty to know, to utter, and to argue freely according to conscience, above all liberties."
John Milton, Areopagitica

HP

LONDON:
THE HAMPDEN PRESS
MMXVIII

Freedom of Speech in England: Its Present State and Likely Prospects, by Sean Gabb

© Sean Gabb, 2013

All rights reserved. No part of this publication may be reproduced, stored in any form or by any means, electronic, mechanical, photocopying, recording or otherwise, without the prior permission of the publisher.

Any person who does any unauthorised act in relation to this publication may be liable to criminal prosecution and civil claims for damages.

First edition, August 2013
Second edition, February 2018

The right of Sean Gabb to be identified as the author of this work has been asserted hereby in accordance with the Copyright, Designs and Patents Act 1988.

Published by
The Hampden Press
73 Middle Street
Deal
Kent CT14 6HN

Telephone: 07956 472 199
E-mail: *sean@seangabb.co.uk*
Web: *www.seangabb.co.uk*

ISBN-13: 978-1985203938
ISBN-10: 1985203936

British Library Cataloguing in Publication Data: A catalogue record for this book is available from the British Library

Contents

INTRODUCTION I

THE CASE AGAINST SEX CENSORSHIP:
A CONSERVATIVE VIEW (1992) 1

OBITUARY, DAVID ALEC WEBB (2012) 30

REFLECTIONS ON THE GARY GLITTER CASE (1999) 34

ON GOLLIWOGS, ONE-EYED SCOTTISH IDIOTS,
AND SENDING POO THROUGH THE POST (2009) 41

YASMIN ALIBHAI-BROWN AND HUMOUR:
NO LAUGHING MATTER (2010) 49

REFLECTIONS ON THE CASE OF SUBHAAN YOUNIS (2005) ... 54

HOW NOT TO STOP THE LONDON BOMBINGS:
IN DEFENCE OF LIBERAL DEMOCRACY (1999) 60

THE LATEST SHOOTINGS IN AMERICA:
AN ENGLISH VIEW (2011) 66

THOUGHTS ON EMMA WEST: HOW TO ARGUE
WITH THE RULING CLASS (2011) 71

EMMA CHAMBERLAIN AND THE ASTOR THEATRE:
HOW DISSIDENTS ARE TREATED IN MODERN ENGLAND
(2006) 77

ON CONVERSING WITH THE BRITISH NATIONAL PARTY
(2005) 83

MORE ON THE PERSECUTION OF THE BNP (2007) 90

THE BRITISH STATE V THE BNP: THE POST-MODERN
TYRANNY
OF "HUMAN RIGHTS" (2009) 95

NEWS FROM THE BRITISH POLICE STATE:
EQUALITY BY DECREE! (2010) 100

PUTTING A NAIL IN THE FUSE BOX: THE PERSECUTION
OF THE BRITISH NATIONAL PARTY (2010) 104

JOHN STUART MILL, THE BNP, AND THE UK'S
DYING DEMOCRACY (2011) 110

DEFENDING THE RIGHT TO DENY THE HOLOCAUST—ONE (1996) 120

DEFENDING THE RIGHT TO DENY THE HOLOCAUST—TWO (2007) 124

REVIEW OF A PRESS LICENSING BILL (1993) 129

STATE REGULATION OF THE BRITISH PRESS:
   SO WHAT? (2012) 133

TO THE READER 139

INDEX 141

I dedicate this book to the Campaign Against Censorship

INTRODUCTION

This book is a collection of essays in defence of freedom of speech, written and published between 1992 and 2012. Instead of by date, I have arranged the essays in loose thematic order. Since my political views have barely changed since I was a boy, I see no problem in such an arrangement. It allows a reasonably smooth exposition of my views. It also gives emphasis to my claim that freedom of speech ought to be defended as a consistent whole, regardless of who is saying what. Even so, these are twenty essays, written over many years, each one addressing a specific issue. I think it would be useful for this Introduction to give a short and connected overview of what I believe.

A Case for Freedom of Speech

I believe in the freedom to publish anything that is not a trespass against some legitimate private right, or that does not clearly and immediately endanger the survival of my country. I should not be free to reveal your private confessions to me of inadequacy; or to publish your own work under my name; or to tell people you are a shoplifter if you are not one; or to say that treasure beyond value is buried six feet below your flowerbeds. I should not be free, in time of war, or in reasonable prospect of war, to publish my government's defence plans. I will also mention the contempt of court laws, and contractual agreements to remain silent. I know that the laws covering these particular trespasses have often been stretched from protection to censorship. I know very well that laws to protect state secrecy will, unless tightly drawn and continuously monitored, be made into a device to cover up various kinds of wrongdoing. But I see no difficulty with the principle of such laws, so long as they only serve their stated purpose. Outside their proper range, there should be no limits on what may be published.

For libertarians, this may be no more than a special case of the general principle that we should be free to do with ourselves and our property as we please. There are difficulties with this principle, of self-ownership. When does a child become an autonomous person? What kinds of property, and modes of acquisition, should be regarded as legitimate?

Since virtually everything we do has some effect on others, where should the boundaries be drawn between free use of oneself and abuse of others? But, these difficulties being settled in any of the usual ways, freedom of speech becomes just another application of the principle. You have the right to buy a computer, and to create on its hard disk whatever you like. You have the right to pass this to anyone else by mutual consent. Your right to freedom of speech is of exactly the same kind as your right to start a window cleaning business, or to dye your hair green, or to make bets on the future price of corn, or to change sex. You may find it convenient, now and again, to claim a "right" to freedom of speech. But this is never more than a derivation from the one true right, which is to self-ownership.

Even with its meaning settled, however, self-ownership is a defence of limited value. In the first place, not everyone else is a libertarian. People who believe in a minimum wage and drug prohibition, or who like heavy taxes on others and lavish state spending on "public services," are unlikely to think much in practice of the self-ownership principle.

In the second place, self-ownership does not, in itself, imply toleration. Whoever does accept it must oppose censorship by the state, or other aggressions against the free use of property. But he is not required to shrug and look the other way if those he can influence say something he finds disagreeable. If he is an employer, he can sack people whose religious or political views are different from his own—even if these views are stated wholly off the job. If he is a landlord, he can evict dissenting tenants. He can organise boycotts of people and businesses. So long as he does not positively aggress against others, he can be a most unpleasant and effective bigot. There would, in a libertarian society, be no shortage of other working arrangements and places to live. But finding these is never free of opportunity cost; and it is conceivable that a libertarian society that accepted only the self-ownership principle would be generally hostile to individuality in the arts and sciences and in daily life. This is not the same as burning people at the stake, or herding them into concentration camps. There would always be the option for like-minded dissidents to form their own communities. The point I am making, though, is that libertarians have no inherent duty to be open-minded, or to tolerate things they do not like.

My preferred defence of freedom of speech, therefore, is the formally separate argument of social utility. I agree with John Stuart Mill that truth and progress are best served by the active toleration of all opinions, no

Introduction

matter how odd or offensive others may find them.[1] His argument comprises two basic claims.

First, an opinion universally held in our own time and place may be false, and an apparently false opinion may be true. There are few of us who did not once believe things that we now reject. There are many instances of presently received opinions laughed at and their discoverers persecuted. Galileo died under house arrest for asserting that the Earth went round the Sun. The German National Socialists drove physicists into exile or idleness for refusing to denounce the "Jewish" myth of the interchangeability of energy and matter. The Soviet Socialists killed those biologists who denied, against Lysenko, that acquired characteristics in living things were transmissible to the next generation.

Leaving aside state persecution, there must be thousands more instances where opinions now received have been rejected, for seemingly good reasons, by men of learning and ability. I think of Wegener's theory of continental drift, or the bacterial cause of many stomach ulcers, or the slow demolition, between the first appearance of syphilis and Pasteur's investigation of microbes, of the miasma theory of epidemics. There are many more received opinions waiting to be overthrown—sometimes by new opinions, sometimes by the reinstatement of what they replaced. Perhaps much cancer is caused by viral infections. Perhaps homosexuality is indeed a mental illness. Perhaps the world is not, after all, more than a few thousand years old.

We can never be sure about any claim that relies on evidence about matters of fact and its interpretation. The more open we are to alternative theories, the closer we are likely to approach to the truth. Moreover, truth, in our civilisation, is not only good in itself. For about three and a half centuries, we have enjoyed a continuous and accelerating improvement in our lives, produced by uncovering the forces of nature and turning these to our benefit.

Second, even if an opinion is false beyond all reasonable doubt, to suppress it is to deprive us or what Mill calls "[a]lmost as great a benefit, the clearer perception and livelier impression of truth, produced by its

---

[1] John Stuart Mill, *Essay On Liberty* (1859), published in *Three Essays by John Stuart Mill*, Oxford University Press, Oxford, 1912. See Chapter II, "Of the Liberty of Thought and Discussion."

Freedom of Speech in England

collision with error."[2] Protect the most solidly based truth with penal laws, and faith in it will insensibly wither.

Take, for instance, a case given by J.A. Froude. Some time around 1860, a school inspector wrote to *The Times*, announcing that, contrary to what every astronomer believed, the Moon did not revolve on its axis. If it did, he explained, it could not always present the same face to us. A few days later, a full answer was published from the Astronomer Royal. The Moon, he explained, did revolve on its axis—but at the same average speed as its orbit about the Earth: only because of these synchronised movements could it always present the same face to us. "[M]ost of us," Froude comments,

> who had before received what the men of science told us with an unintelligent and languid assent, were set thinking for ourselves, and as a result of the discussion, exchanged a confused idea for a clear one.[3]

Yet, suppose the Moon's rotation had been an article of faith, and the Astronomer Royal had been able to answer the inspector with persecution instead of reason—that the inspector had been turned out of his job, or even imprisoned—what then? Froude continues:

> The world outside would have had an antecedent assumption that truth lay with the man who was making sacrifices for it, and that there was little to be said in the way of argument for what could not stand without the help of the law. Everybody could understand the difficulty; not everybody would have taken the trouble to attend to the answer.[4]

If, then, we desire the benefits of progress, we must leave opinions alone. We must leave people to seek out and announce anything that they believe to be true. If we want the occasional gleam of truth, we must put up with an endless torrent of nonsense. We must tolerate it all. We must hope for an answer not in censorship, nor in any other refusal to debate, but in the far greater power of unarmed truth.

Pornography and Experiments of Living

Now, what about pornography? This argument, as normally expressed, covers moral and factual claims. In present terms, it defends the right to

---

[2] *Ibid.*, p.24.

[3] "A Plea for the Free Discussion of Theological Differences" (1863), in *Essays in Literature and History*, by J.A. Froude, "Everyman" edition, J.M. Dent and Co., London, 1906, p. 197.

[4] *Ibid.*

say that there are intellectual differences between the races, or that Islam is a "wicked, vicious faith," or that Theo van Gogh and Lee Rigby got what they deserved, or that the persecution of Jews by the German State between 1933 and 1945 has been exaggerated—or was entirely justified. What then about pornography? The answer is to look again at J.S. Mill. He says that,

> [a]s it is useful that while mankind are imperfect there should be different opinions, so is it that there should be different experiments of living; that free scope should be given to varieties of character, short of injury to others; and that the worth of different modes of life should be proved practically, when any one thinks fit to try them. It is desirable, in short, that in things which do not primarily concern others, individuality should assert itself.[5]

The same considerations apply. If one of these "experiments" turns out to be good, we all gain by it. If it fails, we still gain, so far as we see the value of our established ways. Pornography has many uses. It is an aid to masturbation. It can also encourage sexual experimentation and greater openness about sex and other matters. This latter may be good or bad. The only way to know is to try it, or to watch others try it.

This argument also applies to new kinds of music and art and even clothing and domestic architecture. We are moving away here from pure freedom of speech, into what may be better covered by the phrase "freedom of expression." But, regardless of the self-ownership principle, there is a utilitarian case for most kinds of freedom that I find wholly convincing.

Objections and Replies

The main argument against is to accept the value of free debate in the sciences—something that most of the twentieth century dictatorships most of the time accepted—but to claim that complete freedom of speech is undesirable. We are told that freedom of speech in matters of race and immigration makes people hateful and incites them to violence; and that freedom for pornographers, even when it does not encourage rape and sexual murder, is morally corrupting. Or we are told that "racial hatred" causes measurable distress to the affected groups, or that heterosexual pornography "demeans" women. Hardly anyone nowadays calls for censorship with the old arguments about the need to keep ordinary people

---

[5] John Stuart Mill, *On Liberty*, Chapter III, "Of Individuality, as One of the Elements of Well-Being," *op. cit.*, p.70.

in line. The argument is instead to oppose one set of claims about the public good to another.

I do not accept any of these alternative claims. Once more, I am writing with extreme brevity in an area that has generated libraries of controversy. But I will say the following:

First, there is no easy distinction between scientific and other kinds of speech. Darwinism is more than an argument about the origin of species. Whether they are right or wrong about racial differences, Richard Lynn and Chris Brand are undoubtedly scientific in their methods. So was Francis Galton. A further consideration is that, if the "scientific racists" turn out to be right, the longer term consequences of their work may include the development of technologies to raise all babies to the same high potential.

Second, the claim about incitement rests on a somewhat Pavlovian view of human nature. If someone gathers a mob outside a synagogue or a gay club, and insists that children inside are being murdered, he must take some of the responsibility for any violence that results. He is speaking to people who are not in their proper minds, and he is calling for immediate action to save lives. Let him go on trial for a breach of the peace. But someone who uploads an article or a video to the Internet is in a wholly different position. He is putting arguments that his audience must view as individuals, and with possibly a long time for reflection. If any of those individuals goes out and commits an act of violence, his own judgement and will must be seen as a new intervening cause. The violent individual must bear sole responsibility for his actions. That is in the case where someone has openly called for violence. Mostly, however, incitement is alleged against fairly abstract propositions that require several more stages of argument before they can be seen as a call for violence.

Third, the argument that pornography causes any type of harm is weak. During the past few years, British politicians have been prodded into agreeing that the "sexualisation" of young people is a bad thing, and that something must be done to stop it. The something their prodders have in mind always involves filters or outright blocks on pornography from the Internet.

I could, at this point, turn po-faced, and start citing research papers, as if we were discussing metal fatigue on the railways, or the evolution of spider webs. Instead, I will speak from my own experience. I discovered masturbation when I was rather young, and I was very pleased to lay

Introduction

hands on any material that made it more enjoyable. As soon as I was able—and I regret how long after the first discovery this was—I began having sex with other people. I then found pornography useful both for stimulation and as a menu of suggestions and an instruction guide. Forty years later, I have still not raped or murdered anyone. None of my numerous faults as a person has an evidently sexual cause.

The very limited exposure I had to pornography before I was old enough to make use of it tells me that prepubescent children are incapable of being "sexualised" in any meaningful sense. When I look back on my youth, I resent the lack of "sexualisation" I was able to achieve. I envy young people today, who are never more than a few clicks of the mouse away from whatever takes their fancy, and whose sexual availability to each other would have been one of my more unlikely youthful fantasies. I envy them, but do not wish to send them back to the 1970s. If this is a bad "experiment of living," let the evidence be fairly produced.

Except I am more honest about it, I do not think my own experience is unique. Most people have been masturbating since they were young. Most have been using whatever pornography they like and can obtain. Hardly anyone commits a rape. Even fewer commit sexual murders. I am told that Myra Hindley and Ian Brady read the Marquis de Sade before they began murdering children. I read him too when I was their age. I also watched Pasolini's *Salò*, which they did not—and, I repeat, I am neither a rapist nor a murderer. There may be a connection between pornography and sexual assault. If so, the causal sequence is the opposite of what is usually claimed. People who are already inclined to sexual assault will be drawn to violent pornography. All the evidence I have seen for the contrary view is self-serving claims by convicted sexual criminals. Faced with execution or a lifetime in prison, of course they will plead that their responsibility was diminished by the pornography they used. I cannot blame them for saying this. But I will blame those who believe them.

Fourth, there seems to be a stronger correlation between religious and political writings and acts of violence. This is to be expected. On the one hand, while most people are unwilling to hurt others for their own pleasure, they can turn violent if they believe it is for the greater good. On the other hand, even those who do not themselves turn violent may tolerate violent acts by others for this alleged greater good. This much being allowed, there is the argument, given above, about the nature of incitement. People usually have a reasonable time to choose how they respond to ideas.

Then there is always an inconsistency about calls for censorship. It may be that allowing books like *Mein Kampf* and *The Protocols of the Learned Elders of Zion* to circulate makes people more anti-semitic than they would otherwise be, and that this raises the chance of a *pogrom*. Well, the German national socialists may have murdered ten million non-combatants. How many murders have been inspired by the works of Karl Marx? Fifty million? A hundred million? Why call for suppressing one kind of political writing, and not others that may have led to consequences five or ten times greater? And how many murders—the Crusades and the Inquisition and the Wars of Religion, to mention only Christianity—have been called for by religious texts and religious leaders? When the founders of Aldous Huxley's *Brave New World* outlawed all religion and destroyed all art, they were monstrous yet consistent in their scheme of everlasting peace. The moral crusaders who presently call for censorship are suspiciously inconsistent. They seem concerned less about violent behaviour than to suppress rival excuses for it.

Fifth, the whole argument about how certain published items "hurt" or "demean" is at best worthless psychobabble. If some Moslems were really upset by *The Satanic Verses*, no one was forcing them to buy copies and read it. If its mere existence upset them, they should have called on the Wrath of God—that, or they should have asked if they had not settled in the wrong country.

Otherwise, allowing this nature of hurt to give rise to prosecution opens the way to a complete ending of freedom as we have known it. If sensibilities hurt by the publication of a book can justify legal action, what about someone who claims he is "hurt" by the homosexuals living down the road? Or by the people next door who may be using birth control pills or a dildo? Or by the man who never invites black children to his son's birthday party?

As for the feminists and Christians who complain how women are "demeaned" by pornography, the women who show their bodies to men are consenting adults, and usually well-paid for their work. And there are many women who enjoy pornography as much as men do. No one has—or should have—the right to decide what is good for other adults.

Introduction

What about the Children?

Where sex and pornography are concerned, there is the argument about children. I agree that, below a certain age—I am not sure what age this is, but might accept sixteen as a working assumption—people should not be regarded as adults, and should receive special protection by the law. It should be illegal for older people to have sex with children. It should be illegal to create and publish plainly sexual material that involves children. This being said, I would add the following:

First, I doubt that the amount of unambiguous child pornography is very large. The claims are made: the methodology is never given. In 2004, I went on the BBC against someone from a charity that had recently claimed there were 35,000 paedophile images uploaded every six weeks. I asked these questions: Who was counting the images? Were they newly-created, or recycled from the past? What was meant by a "paedophile image"? Was it children under the age of twelve? Or under the age of 24? How many of these were what the law calls "pseudo-images"—which are assembled from different sources, and in which no children may have been required to pose in any overtly sexual manner, or to take part at all?[6] Were they of 35,000 individuals, or sets of pictures

---

[6] The law is consolidated in section 62 of the Coroners and Justice Act 2009:

Possession of prohibited images of children.

(1) It is an offence for a person to be in possession of a prohibited image of a child.

(2) A prohibited image is an image which—

(a) is pornographic,

(b) falls within subsection (6), and

(c) is grossly offensive, disgusting or otherwise of an obscene character.

(3) An image is "pornographic" if it is of such a nature that it must reasonably be assumed to have been produced solely or principally for the purpose of sexual arousal.

(4) Where (as found in the person's possession) an image forms part of a series of images, the question whether the image is of such a nature as is mentioned in subsection (3) is to be determined by reference to—

(a) the image itself, and

(b) if the series of images is such as to be capable of providing a context for the image) the context in which it occurs in the series of images.

of perhaps a thousand individuals? The answer I got to these questions was a blustering accusation that I was "not taking the issue seriously." You draw your own inference from that.

---

(5) So, for example, where—

(a) an image forms an integral part of a narrative constituted by a series of images, and

(b) having regard to those images as a whole, they are not of such a nature that they must reasonably be assumed to have been produced solely or principally for the purpose of sexual arousal,

the image may, by virtue of being part of that narrative, be found not to be pornographic, even though it might have been found to be pornographic if taken by itself.

(6) An image falls within this subsection if it—

(a) is an image which focuses solely or principally on a child's genitals or anal region, or

(b) portrays any of the acts mentioned in subsection (7). .

(7) Those acts are—

(a) the performance by a person of an act of intercourse or oral sex with or in the presence of a child;

(b) an act of masturbation by, of, involving or in the presence of a child;

(c) an act which involves penetration of the vagina or anus of a child with a part of a person's body or with anything else;

(d) an act of penetration, in the presence of a child, of the vagina or anus of a person with a part of a person's body or with anything else;

(e) the performance by a child of an act of intercourse or oral sex with an animal (whether dead or alive or imaginary);

(f) the performance by a person of an act of intercourse or oral sex with an animal (whether dead or alive or imaginary) in the presence of a child.

(8) For the purposes of subsection (7), penetration is a continuing act from entry to withdrawal.

(9) Proceedings for an offence under subsection (1) may not be instituted—

(a) in England and Wales, except by or with the consent of the Director of Public Prosecutions;

(b) in Northern Ireland, except by or with the consent of the Director of Public Prosecutions for Northern Ireland.

Introduction

By the way, when I asked about the ages of these alleged children, I spoke from experience. In 1995, I went on television to discuss drug relegalisation, and found myself against someone who said he was helping young people as young as thirteen to come off drugs. Suspicious at his use of the phrases "young people" and "as young as," I asked how old some of his cases were. He prevaricated, trying to draw debate back to the youngest age. I pressed and pressed. At last, he mumbled that some of them were 24. The debate collapsed, leaving me in triumph. I accept that he may have been helping children of thirteen, but his odd definition of young people raised obvious suspicions about the numbers he was so fluently citing.

Second, I have seen too many uses of the "saving the kiddies" argument to believe that the campaigners against child pornography are really worried about children. The tobacco control industry focuses on the alleged harm of cigarettes or cigarette advertising to children. Controls on drinking are increasingly demanded for the alleged sake of the children. The War on Drugs is frequently justified by the need to protect children from smoking crack cocaine. The crusade against child pornography is largely a cover for rolling back the liberalisation of the pornography laws. Why else should it be a crime to possess indecent "pseudo-images" of young people? Why else has a recent law criminalised possession of *line drawings* of children in acts of indecency?[7] Protecting children is very often no more than an excuse for policing the adult imagination.

---

[7] See section 65 of the same Act:

(1) The following apply for the purposes of sections 62 to 64.

(2) "Image" includes—

(a) a moving or still image (produced by any means), or

(b) data (stored by any means) which is capable of conversion into an image within paragraph (a).

(3) "Image" does not include an indecent photograph, or indecent pseudo-photograph, of a child.

(4) In subsection (3) "indecent photograph" and "indecent pseudo-photograph" are to be construed—

(a) in relation to England and Wales, in accordance with the Protection of Children Act 1978 (c. 37), and

Freedom of Speech in England

Third, imaginations do not need policing. Only assaults should be against the law. I have dealt with the general claim that pornography leads to rape and murder. I do not believe there is any difference where child pornography is concerned. Let is be granted that most child molesters are found with indecent pictures of children in their possession. The real question is which way the causality runs. Homosexuals will tend to have gay pornography on their computers. "Whale riders" will collect pictures of fat people. Most people found guilty of possessing child pornography—even those who are quite old—have no history of assaulting children. Choice of pornography does not create sexual tastes. It reflects them. Sexual tastes may be innate. At the least, they are established in early childhood.

Of course, it should be illegal to create and to publish child pornography—and perhaps some animal pornography too. Of course, there should be harsh laws against child pornographers—but not because of the alleged effect on its users, but because the act of creation is itself an assault. Let this be the argument for such laws, and let them be framed solely for the protection of children.

The Proposed Internet Filter

Let me go back, however, to the matter of Internet filters. I am writing this Introduction in the August of 2013, and the British Government is pushing hard for an opt-out filter on all new accounts. The plan is that, from next year, or the year after, anyone who signs up with an Internet service provider will be presented with a default block on child pornography. This is not called censorship, as it will not be imposed by

---

(b) in relation to Northern Ireland, in accordance with the Protection of Children (Northern Ireland) Order 1978 (S.I. 1978/1047 (N.I. 17)).

(5) "Child", subject to subsection (6), means a person under the age of 18.

(6) Where an image shows a person the image is to be treated as an image of a child if—

(a) the impression conveyed by the image is that the person shown is a child, or

(b) the predominant impression conveyed is that the person shown is a child despite the fact that some of the physical characteristics shown are not those of a child.

(7) References to an image of a person include references to an image of an imaginary person.

(8) References to an image of a child include references to an image of an imaginary child.

Introduction

law, but by a "voluntary agreement" among Internet service providers. Also, it will be possible to uncheck the box and to receive the same content as before. But it is expected that most people will not uncheck the box. They will put up with the filter because changing default settings is too much trouble for most people. Or they will put up with it because they fear being put on a list of potential sex offenders and visited by the police every time a woman is raped close by where they live, or every time a child goes missing.

Most of my radio and television debates on sexual censorship are with authoritarian Christians. I always put this point to them:

> You deceive yourself when you think the authorities are fundamentally on your side. The moment you ask for a control to be imposed, you put your trust in people you have never seen, who are not accountable to you, who probably do not share your own values, and who will, sooner or later, use the control you have demanded in ways that you find surprising or shocking.

It is a good debating point, as it avoids the need to use up scarce minutes on air with arguments about freedom that do not touch my opponents. I am surprised it has no place in opposing the filter proposals. The most likely filter now proposed will not even be used as a precedent for other controls. It will automatically cover a range of other material, such as discussions of anorexia nervosa, smoking, drinking, "political extremism," and "esoterica." What this last might cover no one can say for sure. It might cover Rosicrucianism, or ancient or modern paganism, or witchcraft. Already, early versions of the filter that seems to be in mind block access to the Libertarian Alliance Blog.[8]

Perhaps they want the proposals to fail. Or perhaps the Prime Minister and his advisers have overplayed their hand. Leaving aside any technical difficulties that are not relevant here, the proposed block is so general that anyone who does opt out cannot risk being seen as a potential sex offender. Indeed, if it is set up as proposed, almost anyone who uses the Internet for anything but mail order shopping will have no choice but to opt out. This must include most schoolchildren.

The general value of the debating point, though, is that the ruling class in this country has lost interest in sexual censorship for its own sake. On the one hand, the Internet has, over the past twenty years, made the old

---

[8] See John Kersey, "What they don't want you to see online," *The Libertarian Alliance Blog* (*http://libertarianalliance.wordpress.com/*), 9th August 2013.

Freedom of Speech in England

laws unenforceable. On the other hand, child pornography excepted, where the law has come close to lunacy, the ruling class has become more liberal in sexual matters.[9] If the religious authoritarians ever make an overpowering clamour for a return to sexual censorship, it will be allowed only as another excuse for political censorship.

The Growth of a Soft-Totalitarian Police State

During the twenty years covered by these essays, England has become a perceptibly freer country where sexuality and sexual expression are concerned. This is to be welcomed. But it does not mean that speech in general has become more free. Instead, we have moved increasingly towards overtly political censorship. We have already reached the point where it is dangerous to speak on matters of race and immigration—and increasingly, of sexual preference—except as the ruling class allows. Anyone who does speak out of turn can be arrested and charged, and, if convicted, sent to prison. Failing this, there are shadow punishments that range from being made unemployable, to the state abduction of children.

The excuse for this has been the prohibition of "hate." Once we look beneath the soft and caring talk of "diversity," though, the real cause of this new censorship is the old desire of any ruling class to shut down debate on its oppressions. I believe that, during at least the past sixty years, the British ruling class has been trying to insulate itself from any but an imaginary accountability to us. It has done this by governing from behind a fig leaf of international treaties and multinational organisations. The European Union is its main current excuse for making laws without our consent, and enforcing them in ways alien to our traditions. But there is also the Council of Europe, and the United Nations, and NATO, among others. These bodies have no real powers of compulsion. Their workings are heavily influenced by the British Government. Their commands are taken as binding here with only a show of reluctance.

Our rulers have pre-empted opposition to these policies by a deliberate balkanisation of the country. In a free society, there would be some

---

[9] I have already shown how, in the past twenty years, possession of certain images has for the first time been made criminal. The Coroners and Justice Act 2009 criminalised the possession of Japanese Hentai cartoons. At a stroke, millions of people in this country were made into criminals. They were opened to arbitrary raids by the police of the kind so loved by the American authorities. The first victims of the law were the elderly remnants of the Paedophile Information Exchange. Hentai cartoons were "found" on their computers, and they were all sent to prison—one of them with an *indefinite* sentence.

movement of peoples; and many incomers would be alien in their appearance and ways. At the same time, the incomers would have skills desired by the natives, and would find themselves under strong social pressure to conform to—or simply not to challenge—established ways of life. What we have had, however, is a state-sponsored mass-immigration, largely of profoundly alien paupers. State sponsorship has involved generous welfare benefits, and laws compelling association on terms almost wholly favourable to the incomers.

The natural result has been a gathering collapse of liberal democracy. One of the main reasons for this is that a reasonably homogenous nation state may not be democratic, but it *can* be democratic. People who have a common identity will often conceive common interests, and stand together against a government that does not respect these interests. They may also trust each other with political power—confident that differences over economic or other policies will not be carried to the point of civil war.

Let me turn once more to J.S. Mill:

> Free institutions are next to impossible in a country made up of different nationalities. Among a people without fellow-feeling, especially if they read and speak different languages, the united public opinion, necessary to the working of representative government, cannot exist. The influences which form opinions and decide political acts are different in the different sections of the country. An altogether different set of leaders have the confidence of one part of the country and of another. The same books, newspapers, pamphlets, speeches, do not reach them. One section does not know what opinions, or what instigations, are circulating in another. The same incidents, the same acts, the same system of government, affect them in different ways; and each fears more injury to itself from the other nationalities than from the common arbiter, the state. Their mutual antipathies are generally much stronger than jealousy of the government. That any one of them feels aggrieved by the policy of the common ruler is sufficient to determine another to support that policy. Even if all are aggrieved, none feel that they can rely on the others for fidelity in a joint resistance; the strength of none is sufficient to resist alone, and each may reasonably think that it consults its own advantage most by bidding for the favour of the government against the rest.[10]

---

[10] John Stuart Mill, *Considerations on Representative Government* (1861), Chapter XVI, "On Nationality, as Connected with Representative Government," *op. cit.*, p.382.

Freedom of Speech in England

A further twist in the ratchet—and this has been applied by the cultural Marxists who only inherited a set of tendencies already set in motion by the previous ruling class—has been to make all but the most measured complaints about this transformation dangerous. One of the cases discussed in this book is that of Emma West, the South London Tram Lady. When she was first arrested, some people tried to argue that this was purely a breach of the peace. What she had said was that the number of foreigners about her left her unable to believe that she was still in her own country. Because it is still legal to make this point without copying her use of the word "fuck" in its adjectival and adverbial forms, hers could not be seen as a political arrest. But was there any serious chance that any of the people she insulted would have got up from their seats and begun a riot? Would she have been arrested and made into a public villain had she been caught urinating in front of a war memorial? She became a political martyr because she uttered heresy, and because she belonged to a social class in which this heresy is widely shared, and which is considered by our ruling class as more to be feared than a few middle class dissidents.

Not Only the Foreigners

Something not covered in the man text of this book, but worth mentioning here, for the sake of completeness and of honesty, is that the balkanisation of England has involved not only the separatism of highly visible aliens. Black people, Moslems, to some extent Sikhs and Hindus—these are the obvious communities of grievance, all demanding, or encouraged to demand, special consideration. But there are also certain homosexuals. I was shocked when, as a young man, I found that some gay activists had joined in the clamour against "hate." How could it be that men who lived in the shadow of censorship could themselves be calling for censorship?

The answer is that they knew better than I did which way the long term winds were blowing. When I was younger, failure to join in the condemnations of homosexuality could sometimes be socially dangerous. Today, any breath of condemnation can be legally dangerous. The main law used is the Public Order Act 1986. This was not written with homosexuals in mind, but has been reinterpreted by the police and the Crown Prosecution Service, and variously amended by Parliament.[11]

---

[11] The main relevant text is section 5, Harassment, alarm or distress:

(1) A person is guilty of an offence if he—

Introduction

John Kersey has listed the main harassment to the middle of 2013 under the Act:

> Pensioner Harry Hammond, who preached in Bournemouth holding a placard saying "Stop Homosexuality, Stop Lesbianism" was arrested and charged under Section 5 of the Public Order Act in 2001. He was convicted, his placards destroyed, and he died soon afterwards.
>
> Philip Howard, who preached in "hellfire and brimstone" fashion for some years at Oxford Circus, was prosecuted for harassment of a passer-by in 2005, and cleared of all charges. The following year, Westminster Council applied for an ASBO in an attempt to silence him. This being

---

(a) uses threatening, abusive or insulting words or behaviour, or disorderly behaviour, or

(b) displays any writing, sign or other visible representation which is threatening, abusive or insulting,

within the hearing or sight of a person likely to be caused harassment, alarm or distress thereby.

(2) An offence under this section may be committed in a public or a private place, except that no offence is committed where the words or behaviour are used, or the writing, sign or other visible representation is displayed, by a person inside a dwelling and the other person is also inside that or another dwelling.

(3) It is a defence for the accused to prove—

(a) that he had no reason to believe that there was any person within hearing or sight who was likely to be caused harassment, alarm or distress, or

(b) that he was inside a dwelling and had no reason to believe that the words or behaviour used, or the writing, sign or other visible representation displayed, would be heard or seen by a person outside that or any other dwelling, or

(c) that his conduct was reasonable.

(4) A constable may arrest a person without warrant if—

(a) he engages in offensive conduct which a constable warns him to stop, and

(b) he engages in further offensive conduct immediately or shortly after the warning.

(5) In subsection (4) "offensive conduct" means conduct the constable reasonably suspects to constitute an offence under this section, and the conduct mentioned in paragraph (a) and the further conduct need not be of the same nature.

(6) A person guilty of an offence under this section is liable on summary conviction to a fine not exceeding level 3 on the standard scale.

Freedom of Speech in England

> granted, he moved to Brixton underground station where I understand he can still be found today.
>
> New Yorker Shawn Holes, preaching in Glasgow, was fined £1,000 after stating that homosexuals are going to Hell.
>
> Stephen Green—now National Director of Christian Voice, a group with much to say on these matters—was arrested for handing out religious leaflets at a gay Mardi Gras festival in Cardiff in 2006; the charges against him were dropped.
>
> In 2008, American preachers Arthur Cunningham and Joseph Abraham handed out leaflets and spoke with local youths in Birmingham. A PCSO, who was later given "corrective training," allegedly told the preachers that if they returned to the predominantly Muslim area they would be beaten up.
>
> The tide really appears to have started to turn with Cumbrian street preacher Dale McAlpine, who was arrested and charged under section 5 of the Public Order Act for stating that homosexuals were acting against the word of God. The charges against him were dropped, and he then won £7,000 plus costs in compensation from the police.
>
> Then Anthony Rollins preached in Birmingham against effeminacy and homosexuality and was arrested and charged; in court he was awarded over £4,000 in damages.
>
> Last year [2012], Bhachoo distributed anti-gay leaflets outside a Tesco store in Kent. His case was dismissed by the magistrates.[12]

Dr Kersey may be right that use of the Act to harass street preachers is falling into contempt. I doubt, however, if the more authoritarian gay activists will give up on their attempt at censorship. This is foolish. Sexual preference is often an important part of personal identity, but hardly ever so pervasive as nationality or religion. It is unlikely to provide the same cohesion as Judaism or Islam, or Englishness. There are no children to give it continuity beyond one generation, nor the belief in God that holds ascetic religious communities together through time. Most of all—despite the relaxed attitude of their main religious texts, and the tolerance of pederasty required by their seclusion of women—Moslems nowadays do not like homosexuality. Their dislike is shared by most other racial and religious minorities. I say that the cry going up from

---

[12] John Kersey, "Time to Stop the Persecution of the Street Preachers," The Libertarian Alliance Blog (*http://libertarianalliance.wordpress.com/*), 5th July 2013.

Introduction

some of the gay activists, for persecution of dissent, is not only wrong in itself, but is both creating precedents for a renewed persecution of homosexuals, and providing excuses for revenge. Homosexuals are the weakest element in our "community of communities." They, above all, should see the moral rightness and the personal advantage in the libertarian call for equality of freedom.[13]

Concluding Remarks

It would once have been highly eccentric to fill a book about freedom of speech with discussions of race and immigration. The earliest essays in this book follow the twentieth century pattern of defending the right to publish and use pornography. But we are where we are. If you really believe in freedom of speech, and you want to write about it, you have no choice now but to defend the rights of Nick Griffin and Emma West and Subhaan Younis, and all the other dissidents in our modern police state. The transformation described above makes it impossible to stay within the safe zone of pornography and sex and to be completely honest. Mass-immigration and political correctness have brought outright political censorship into this country for the first time since the 1790s. It is worse than the 1790s. The panic over the French Revolution eventually passed away. Within a decade, I doubt if anyone will question the need for censorship. We have a police state now because that is what the ruling class wants. We shall soon have one because it will be seen as the only alternative to civil war.

I have explained my belief in freedom of speech in terms both of self-ownership and of social utility. It is a fact, though, that freedom of speech has only ever existed in places where most people have not been very concerned by what is said. Arguments for freedom of worship, or even of conscience, got nowhere in sixteenth century Europe. Toleration only emerged with the growth of philosophical indifference in the later seventeenth century, and became a general policy only once a consensus was established among those who mattered of what state power could and should try to achieve.

Mass-immigration as we know it is destroying the consensus on which toleration so far has rested. We are not there yet, but I can see a time when it will be necessary to lock people like Emma West away, because

---

[13] Of course, I exempt Peter Tatchell from this criticism. Despite his socialism, despite his weakness on freedom of association, his forthright defence of freedom of speech makes him a shining exception to the generality of gay activists.

Freedom of Speech in England

not to do so will lead to rioting in which hundreds die. In the mixed countries of South Asia, competitive rioting is an accepted means of getting advantages for one community over another. The need to keep the rioting within limits justifies repressive policing. The need to avoid rioting justifies various formal and informal schemes of censorship. As the Islamic population of this country grows in numbers and confidence, there will be further controls on the advertising and displays of alcohol, and then of pork; and natives will be pressured into covering up in Islamic areas. There will be a renewed censorship of sexual representation. There will be stricter prohibitions of adverse comment on Islam and matters of Islamic concern. As the native population grows more sullen and more tribal, we shall demand and receive censorship of adverse comment on us.

I suspect that such freedom of non-sexual speech as we enjoyed until recently will not be recovered. I suspect that such freedom of speech as we currently enjoy will diminish further. If this book gains any circulation above the trivial or ephemeral, it may be regarded less as a demand for freedom of speech in England than as its obituary.

THE CASE AGAINST SEX CENSORSHIP:
A CONSERVATIVE VIEW (1992)[14]

When in the autumn of 1990 I helped form Conservatives Against Sex Censorship, I never supposed that I was setting out on a fast or an easy campaign. Granted, the Party leaders had for years been talking of freedom with all the apparent fervour of a convert.[15] Granted, the Party was filled at every level with adulterers, paedophiles, sado-masochistic leather worshippers and enthusiastic users of pornography. Even so, it had also proclaimed itself the Party of "Family Values"; and

---

[14] This chapter is a revised version of my speech to the NCROPA fringe meeting at the 1992 Conservative Party Conference at Brighton. It was first published in 1992 as Political Notes No. 70, ISBN 1 85637 122 0, by the Libertarian Alliance, London.

It originally began with this dedication: "I wish here to record my thanks to David Webb, Secretary of the National Campaign for the Reform of the Obscene Publications Acts (NCROPA), for his assistance in the CASC campaign. David has been running his campaign far longer than any of us; and, in any future account of the rearguard actions against the puritan onslaught since the 1970s, David's name will be prominently mentioned." For more about David, see the next essay in this book.

[15] See, for example, John Major: "At the heart of our philosophy is a determination to reinstate the individual to his or her rightful place in society. To offer him new incentives and opportunities to use his initiative. To deploy his talents. To demand something of him. To enable him to achieve something for himself and his family. And to take control of his own life....

[The role of government] is to take the steps which will enable people to help themselves. Left to their own devices, people will create a spontaneous, well-ordered society....

Our appeal is unashamedly populist. Quite simply, it is that people know best. That they should choose for themselves, and not have the choices made for them by politicians, self-styled experts, or, for want of a better word, the establishment" (From a speech given to the Radical Society in late 1989—quoted, T*he Sunday Times*, London, 2nd December, 1990).

whatever these things actually were, the right to look at frank portrayals of the sexual act was not among them.

Accordingly, I was neither surprised nor disappointed to read in the 1992 Manifesto that

> [w]e have the toughest anti-pornography laws in Western Europe, and we will keep them that way.[16]

I take this not as an indication of failure, but as an incentive to work harder. Even if it may not be possible in the short term to end these hypocritical shifts among the leadership, we shall certainly be able to let the public know that on pornography, as on the Maastricht Treaty and on the closing of coal mines, the Conservative Party does not always speak with a single voice.

As part of this greater effort, I begin by rehearsing some of the arguments against the suppression of pornography, and describe some of the laws by which the Government continues to try suppressing it.

The Case against Suppression

Now, I might, in common with some other liberals, try to get by here with a straightforward syllogism. I am a classical liberal. A belief in free speech is a part of classical liberalism. Pornography is speech. Therefore, there should be no controls on the publication of pornography.

Speech and Non-Speech

I do not accept this syllogism. It does apply to much that has, and that might, be considered pornographic. *Lady Chatterley's Lover* by D.H. Lawrence, *The Well of Loneliness* by Radcliffe Hall, the novels of William Burroughs and John Rechy—these have all to some extent been classed as obscene. I have no doubt that many of them have been found sexually arousing by some people. But they are also speech. Each propagates, with varying degrees of success, a certain view of life and how it is to be achieved or defended. Pasolini's *Salò* and Rainer Werner Fassbinder's *Querelle* both come also within this category, together with many other films. So too do many statues and paintings. J.P. David's *Rape of the Sabine Women*, for example, and the *Tyrannoctonoi* of Critias and Nesiotes, both represent nudity. One, indeed, represents two

---

[16] *The Best Future for Britain: The Conservative Manifesto*, 1992, Conservative Central Office, London, 1992, p. 31.

nude homosexual lovers, one of whom was considerably below the age of twenty one. But each work of art, what ever other use it may allow, is undeniably a political statement. There are, of course, many other masterpieces of Western art, any one of which might be regarded by someone as arousing, and by someone else as indecent, but that are also statements of certain ideals that cannot be reduced to any simple message—or even properly to words.

But the word "pornography" also covers things that cannot really be classed as speech. Frederick Schauer hypothesises an extreme example of "hard core pornography." He imagines a film ten minutes long that consists of nothing but close shots of the genitals of a man and woman while performing the sexual act. The film is shown to paying customers who either experience spontaneous orgasm or are led to masturbate. He argues

> that any definition of 'speech'... that included this film in this setting is being bizarrely literal or formalistic. There are virtually no differences in intent and effect from the sale of a plastic or vibrating sex aid, the sale of a body through prostitution, or the sex act itself. At its most extreme, hard core pornography is a sex aid, no more and no less, and the fact that there is no physical contact is only fortuitous.[17]

I agree with Dr Schauer. To bring all pornography under the principle of free speech is to weaken that principle by expanding it beyond what it can reasonably cover. It is also to put up a defence of pornography too weak to be sustained. Though it can stand by itself—and ought in our everyday practice to be regarded as standing by itself—the principle of free speech is, to a consistent liberal, a specific application of a more general principle. That principle is the right of adult human beings to run their own lives—a right limitable only by the need to protect the equal rights of others. To show a film that does nothing but portray a sexual act may not be speech, but is still a use of freedom.

It is also a beneficial use of freedom. Sex is good. It is good as part of a loving relationship. It is good in itself. Thinking about it is obviously good. For many whom emotional or physical circumstances restrain from forming any relationships, there is no alternative to masturbating while thinking about it or watching representations of it. At the very worst,

---

[17] Frederick Schauer, *Free Speech: A Philosophical Enquiry*, Cambridge University Press, 1982, p. 181.

Freedom of Speech in England

there are some people whose tastes are such that they should be positively encouraged to satisfy them through solitary means.

Pornography, then, is to be defended because it is a use of freedom. It is to be seen as good because it contributes to human happiness—or at least may relieve misery.

National Decline

There are two standard arguments against this point of view. The first is that pornography in some way rots the moral fibre of the nation. It produces an increase in the number and variety of sexual relationships. And an excess of pleasure, according to some people, leads through personal enervation to national decline. Take, for example, Mr C. Hill:

> It is worth remembering that of the 27 civilisations the world has so far known each one has collapsed through moral disorder and corruption.... The same fate will overtake Britain in the near future with the systematic perversion of our children and the corrupt personal morals of large numbers of our citizens.[18]

This type of reasoner usually points to the selfless restraint of our ancestors who built the British Empire, and compare this with the Romans, whose private vices brought on the collapse of their empire.

The argument is not always pitched quite so crudely. But, however well-expressed and qualified, it is factually wrong. There is no necessary disjunction between sexual licence and great achievement. The evidence points in quite the opposite direction. Latin literature began its golden age during the lifetime of Catullus. His excellence in the simpler lyric metres was never rivalled by any other Roman poet. His obscenity has led to the omission of at least one of his pieces from every edition annotated for use in the schools.[19] The Roman Empire reached its greatest

---

[18] Address to the Order of Christian Unity, in *New Humanism*, Autumn 1984—quoted, W. Thompson and J. Annetts, *Soft-Core: A Content Analysis of Legally Available Pornography in Britain 1968-90 and the Implications of Aggression Research*, Published at Reading University, September 1990, p. 32.

[19] For my readers' edification, I hereby supply this omission:

> *Paedicabo ego uos et irrumabo*
> *Aureli pathice et cinaede Furi*
> *qui me ex uersiculis meis putastis*
> *quod sunt molliculi parum pudicum.*
> *Nam castum esse decet pium poetam*
> *ipsum uersiculos nihil necesse est*

The Case against Sex Censorship: A Conservative View

geographical expansion during the lifetimes of Juvenal and Martial. Though each is different in his tone, both describe a moral climate that makes Berlin during the Weimar Republic look rather tame. Only after the authorities had become more puritan did the Empire begin its decline.[20]

Our own greatness was not founded on restraint. There were extremes of continence; but everyone knows how the Victorians made sexual hypocrisy into a system. Families were large. The cities teemed with prostitutes of both sexes. The criminal laws against immorality, though more colourful than our own, were scarcely more strictly enforced. For those who were cramped in England, the colonies offered endless opportunities. How these were used is described in a most interesting book by Ronald Hyams.[21] As soon as they were suppressed, the light of

---

> *qui tum denique habent salem ac leporem*
> *si sunt molliculi ac parum pudici*
> *et quod pruriat incitare possunt*
> *non dico pueris sed his pilosis*
> *qui duros nequeunt mouere lumbos.*
> *Vos qui milia multa basiorum*
> *legistis male me marem putastis?*
> *Paedicabo ego uos et irrumabo*
> (Catullus, *Poem* XVI).

> I'll fuck your arses and give you my cock to suck,
> Passive-positioned Aurelius and rent-boy Furius,
> who think me indecent because of my decadent verses.
> For while the poet himself ought to be pure,
> his works are another matter—which works,
> undeniably elegant and charming
> (even if decadent and indecent)
> and able to set the lustful going,
> I address not to boys but to hairy brutes
> who just aren't up to pelvic thrusts.
> Do you, who read about my "many thousand kisses,"
> think me a bad man?
> I'll fuck your arses and give you my cock to suck.

[20] On this point see John Boswell, *Christianity, Social Tolerance and Homosexuality: Gay People in Western Europe from the Beginning of the Christian Era to the Fourteenth Century*, University of Chicago Press, London, 1980.

[21] *Empire and Sexuality: The British Experience*, Manchester University Press, 1990. Take, for example, this extract from the 137 page verse autobiography of Kenneth Searight, a "dashing young officer" and defender of the Raj:

Freedom of Speech in England

genius began to fade from our imperial administration. At home, our greatest age of moral purity—the first half of this century—coincided with our fall from greatness.[22]

> And now the scene shifted and I passed
> From sensuous Bengal to fierce Peshawar
> An Asiatic stronghold where each flower
> Of boyhood planted in its restless soil
> is—*ipso facto*—ready to despoil
> (or be despoiled by) someone else; the yarn
> Indeed so has it that the young Pathan
> Thinks it peculiar if you would pass
> Him by without some reference to his arse.
> Each boy of certain age will let on hire
> His charms to indiscriminate desire,
> To wholesale Buggery and perverse letches....
> To get a boy was easier than to pick
> The flowers by the wayside; for as quick
> As one went out another one came in....
> Scarce passed a night but I in rapturous joy
> Indulged in mutual sodomy, the boy
> Fierce-eyed, entrancing....
> And when his luscious bottom-hole would brim
> Full of my impoured essenses, we'd change
> The role of firing point (but not the range)
> Until his catapult, e'er strongly charged,
> The target with a hail of sperm enlarged.
> Then half an hour... and back again I'd come
> To plunge my weapon in his drenching bum
> (p. 131).

Take again: "Some of the early London Missionary Society missionaries in Tahiti slept with Tahitian women. Some defected from the mission for Tahitian or Tongan women, among them B. Broomhall, T. Lewis and G. Vason, the latter taking several wives. Sex was pressed upon the missionaries. Mostly they resisted, but their children often did not, finding the pervasive sensuousness of the South Seas most enjoyable. Missionaries soon aimed to send their children back to Britain for their education, in order to reduce their 'premature' exposure to sex." (*ibid*, p. 103).

[22] Prudery, of course, did not wholly conquer the Empire. "Perhaps the most ambivalent and controversial eccentric in the African episcopate was Canon W.G. Lucas, first Bishop of Masasi, 1926-44, who was responsible for pioneering (several years earlier) a Christian jando or initiation ceremony for boys in their early teens. It was a seriously thought-out attempt to formulate a syncretistic rite, but the combination of circumcision and confirmation was rejected by most other missionaries as 'little better than an orgy', although, as Ranger points out, the local

I do not seek to draw any causal scheme from these correlations. I mention them only to show the feebleness of this type of argument.

Sexual Crimes

The second argument is more simple. Pornography, we are told, encourages coercive sexual aggression. Not even Mary Whitehouse, or her "feminist" sisters, would claim that everyone who reads or watches pornography will become another Myra Hindley or Ted Bundy. But it is claimed that there are some weak-minded people whose inhibitions may be temporarily overborne, or who may become persuaded that women and even children are legitimate targets—whether or not they consent, whether or not the law permits. If this were so, there might well be a case for legal control, in order to protect the equal rights of others. For once freedom become unequal in this respect, it is transformed at once into power—and into power of the worst kind.

There is a vast empirical literature on this point. Some studies conclude that there is an encouragement to crime. Others claim that there is none, or that pornography may discourage by its cathartic effect. Others come to no firm conclusion either way. For myself, I doubt that there is a causal link. The most recent official study, commissioned by the Home Office, and costing £650,000, supports my doubt. Its authors, Dr Guy Cumberbatch of Aston University and Dr Dennis Howett of the University of Loughborough, urge further research, but deny the existence of any obvious causal link. They find that

> sexual crimes and violent sexual crimes may be carried out by people who seem to have a special interest in certain kinds of pornography....

> [But] [t]he evidence does not point to pornography as a cause of deviant sexual orientation in offenders. Rather, it seems to be used as part of that deviant sexual orientation....

> It is unlikely that pornography is the only determinant of sexual and other forms of violence, and that pornography can be influential in the absence of other conducive factors....

> It is known that exposure to such material is common in later childhood and adolescence, but apart from reports of children used in producing

---

people liked it. Lucas (without a hint of irony) claimed that 'a wonderful opportunity is given in this way to the Christian priest of getting into real personal touch with his boys'. He put 700 boys through this rewarding ritual, but had no plans to extend it to girls. Clitoridectomy posed problems too daunting even for a High Anglican Bishop" (*ibid*, pp. 105-6).

pornography or exposed to pornography as part of sexual abuse, little evidence exists that pornography is harmful.

Indeed, evidence exists that exposure to pornography relatively later in life than normal is more likely to be associated with sexual problems....[23]

Even, moreover, if some definite link could be established between pornography and coercive sexual aggression, there would remain one very strong reason for not taking action against it. That reason is freedom of speech. I am dealing here only with that sort of pornography that can be brought under the heading of speech. I recall it claimed somewhere that the murders committed by Myra Hindley and Ian Brady were partly inspired by reading the works of the Marquis de Sade. I recall it equally claimed that the murders committed by Gilles de Rais in the high middle ages were partly inspired by reading *caps. lxiii-iv* of the *Vita Tiberii* of Suetonius. If this really be so, are we to prohibit de Sade and censor Suetonius? The former is a key figure in the history of the French Enlightenment. He was a major influence on Baudelaire and Swinburne, to name only two great poets of the following century. Interspersed among all the whippings and brandings in his works, there is a moral philosophy that can be used to attack the utilitarianism of which it is more than a parody. Suetonius is, with Tacitus and to a lesser extent Dio Cassius, our best remaining narrative source for the first century of the Roman Empire. The offending chapter is either omitted from most translations, or left in its original Latin. But it is of great historical importance.[24] There are many other works against which the same charge may be laid and the same defence made.

---

[23] Quoted, *The Daily Telegraph*, London, 21st December, 1990. See also Thompson and Annetts, *op. cit. supra*.

[24] Therefore, I translate some of it from Latin: "Having settled on Capri, Tiberius had a special room fitted out for his secret debaucheries, in which selected groups of girls and well-hung youths practised monstrous forms of intercourse. These forms he called 'spintrian postures'. In one of them, the young people would form a triplet, and so give themselves up to mutual defilements in his presence, so reviving by the sight of this his waning passions....

"His turpitude went still further, to such disgusting lengths that they can scarcely be described. He had little children, barely weaned from their mothers, taught to play between his legs as he swam in his bath. He called them his little fishes on account of how they would bite and lick him, and to fellate him as though they were still taking suck from their mothers. To such pleasures had age and inclination disposed him."

The Case against Sex Censorship: A Conservative View

To alter the charge somewhat, how many murders have been inspired by the works of Karl Marx? Fifty million? A hundred million? Who knows? For every one man or woman whose imagination may have boiled over from reading about the Imperial orgies on Capri, there must have been a hundred fanatics sent out of control from reading *The Communist Manifesto*. For every woman and child left dead or bleeding by a lone attacker, there must have been thousands murdered during the Stalin Terror. Every argument against de Sade and those like him can be intensified a hundredfold against Karl Marx. And Karl Marx, whatever else may be said against him, is perhaps the one writer who must be read if any sense is to be made of our often catastrophic century.[25]

Think, yet again, of the *Bible*. Christianity may truly be a religion of peace and freedom. Until around two centuries ago, it was regarded as anything but that. From its first establishment by Constantine, in the third century, until the triumph of that school headed by Voltaire, in the eighteenth century, its most prominent divines believed no less firmly in the mission of Jesus Christ than in the absolute duty of the magistrate to seek out and punish the smallest hint of religious non-conformity. There were the Arian and Monophysite and Monothelite controversies. There was the crusade against the Albigenses. There were the Reformation and Counter-Reformation. There were the wars of religion. There was the ruthless—and, to our minds, the insane—persecution of witches. It is impossible to calculate even the number of lives destroyed by Christian enthusiasm, let alone the quantity of misery created by it. It is, however, easily comparable with Marxist-Leninism as one of the great scourges of humanity. The single text, "Compel them to come in,"[26] has inspired more violence than the whole vast mass of the pornography that sends the National Viewers' and Listeners' Association into paroxysms of outrage and terror. Are we on that account to suppress the Bible?

I might also say that the most horrifying sexual crimes have been committed by men for whom no connection has been alleged or proved

---

[25] Even so, it is well-known how works far more valuable than anything by Marx have been attacked for some alleged immoral tendency. Thus, W.H. Lecky on a charge made against Linnaeus: "Some good people in Sweden desired, it is said, to have his system of botany suppressed, because it was based upon the discovery of the sexes of the plants, and was therefore calculated to inflame the minds of youth." (*History of the Rise and Influence of the Spirit of Rationalism in Europe* (1865), Watts & Co., London, 1946, Part II, p. 16, note 8).

[26] *Luke*, 14:23.

Freedom of Speech in England

with pornography. There was Peter Sutcliffe, the "Yorkshire Ripper," who claimed to have killed in obedience to direct instructions from God Almighty. Only recently, I have read of the case of Andrei Chikatilo, "believed to be this century's most prolific and sadistic mass killer." I quote from my newspaper report:

> He has already admitted killing and raping most of the [fifty three] victims, many boys and girls as young as eight. He is accused of prolonging their death agonies to derive maximum pleasure.

> No clue was left behind at the scene of the crimes, except for a mutilated and disembowelled corpse. Body parts were missing, cut out or bitten off. Sexual organs were eaten and incisions made in the eyes.[27]

I have so far read nothing of any supposed "addiction" to hard-core pornography. I shall, indeed, be surprised to hear of any. The former Soviet Union had controls on pornography that even Mary Whitehouse might think sufficient.

Pornography, then, cannot be claimed a sufficient or even a necessary reason for the commission of sexually violent crimes.

The Law

As the Manifesto boasts, our laws on pornography really are, with the possible exception of the Irish Republic—which was until 1922 part of the United Kingdom any way—the most repressive in the European Economic Community and in the English-speaking world. The Police are able, on a Magistrate's warrant, to seize anything that they consider "obscene." The Defendant can have the matter taken into court and argued before a Jury. But there is not, and never has been, an objective test of obscenity. The Jury is not called on to decide a question of fact, but of opinion. It must decide whether the item before it is such as to tend to deprave and corrupt those likely to be brought in contact with it. To this indefinably vague test, nearly the whole of everything we read, listen to or look at is subject.

Until 1959, the law was more repressive. Before then, not one of the novels mentioned above was legally available in this country. *Lady Chatterley's Lover* was available in a version from which all fourteen graphic depictions of sex and all the naughty words had been carefully Bowdlerised. *The Well of Loneliness* had been suppressed in 1928 on

---

[27] "Sadistic Russian Serial Killer Faces Death Sentence," *The Daily Telegraph*, London, 14th October 1992.

account of just one sentence—"And that night they were not divided"—that hinted at a lesbian relationship.[28] Pornography had always been for sale on the black market; and the titles alone of some Victorian works remain as curious reminders of what our ancestors found exciting.[29] But the law was strict. Publication was a criminal offence carrying both fines and imprisonment.

There is no law of film censorship in itself in Great Britain. But the Cinematograph Acts 1909 and 1952 allow local authorities to require a licence to be taken out before any premises can be used for showing films to the public. Intended originally to cover fire and other safety regulations, these provisions have long since been used to justify local censorship. The usual practice of the licensing authorities has been to forbid cinema owners to show any film that has not been granted a certificate from the British Board of Film Censors—despite its name, a private body dating from 1913 and run by the film industry. The obscenity laws fully apply to film. But the practice has been not to prosecute where a certificate has been granted. Since the BBFC has always been rather cautious in its granting of certificates, there has been room for the development of private cinema clubs, to show films that have not been certificated, but are probably not within the legal definition of obscene. Those that do come within the definition are liable to forfeiture and destruction, and their distributors to the normal penalties.

Censorship of the theatre began in 1551, to curb the discussion of religious topics before an illiterate audience. This law fell gradually into abeyance. Another was passed in 1739 by the Walpole Government, to prevent satirical attacks on itself. The Lord Chamberlain was given the power to grant or refuse a licence for any public performance. Unlicensed performances were to be punished by closure of the theatre and imprisonment of the actors. This power was extended by the Theatres Act 1843. Works by Dumas and Ibsen were refused licences, as was

---

[28] In 1974, it was read as a *Book at Bedtime* on BBC Radio 4.

[29] Geoffrey Robertson lists the following: *The New Lady's Tickler* (1860), *Lady Bumtickler's Revels* (1872), *Colonel Spanker's Experimental Lecture* (1879), *The Story of a Dildoe* (1880), *My Secret Life* (1885), *Raped on the Railway: A True Story of a Lady who was First Ravished and Then Flagellated on the Scotch Express* (1894)—see his *Freedom, the Individual and the Law*, Penguin Books, London, 1989, p. 181.

Freedom of Speech in England

Wilde's *Salome*. Even *The Mikado* had its licence withdrawn for a year in 1907, on the occasion of a visit by the Japanese Crown Prince. Before 1968, theatres were prevented from staging any play uncut that mentioned homosexuality, venereal disease or birth control, among much else. In that year, a new Theatres Act was passed that removed the Lord Chamberlain's licensing power, and plays were left subject only to the law of obscenity.[30]

The Obscene Publications Act 1959 was a step in the right direction. It was not intended as a liberal measure. It was announced in its preamble as "an Act to strengthen the law concerning pornography." But its effect was liberal. It divided obscene publications into two categories—pornography and literature. The former was to be hunted down exactly as before. Indeed, aided by a further Act of 1964, the hunt was made easier by giving the authorities greater powers of entry and search. But the latter was to be preserved from suppression. It was left to a Jury, assisted where necessary by expert testimony, to decide whether a publication had or had not sufficient redeeming merit as literature or significance on some other ground to sanction its preservation. For the first time, moreover, it was permitted for a work to be considered as a whole, and not only as a few isolated passages or words.

The first test of the new Act was the celebrated *Lady Chatterley* trial. Looked at after thirty years, the Defence was farcical. Here were the greatest critics in the land, together with an Anglican Bishop, trooping through the witness box to find infinite beauties in an indifferent novel about adultery written by an avowed pagan. But the prosecution failed. Over the next few decades, censorship of the written word insensibly evaporated. In that area, we do have at the moment something like a genuinely free press. During the same time, film censorship has greatly diminished. We are now able to watch what until fairly recently would have had the Police raiding the cinema.

But the censorship of purely pornographic films and picture magazines—of that pornography which cannot rightly be called speech—continues. Articles that may be freely bought and sold in Washington and Paris are illegal in London. For some years, corruption

---

[30] This is not strictly the case. In 1980, Mrs Whitehouse found a loophole in the Act that allowed her to begin a prosecution against the director of Howard Brenton's left wing play *The Romans in Britain* under the Sexual Offences Act 1956, on the grounds that he had allegedly procured an act of "gross indecency between males".

The Case against Sex Censorship: A Conservative View

within the Metropolitan Police ensured their ready availability, if at a price. But that corruption has largely been eradicated. I do not say it has been entirely eradicated. For total honesty in the face of such huge temptation is not possible among any considerable body of men. But the more glaring corruption is no longer visible. The black market still flourishes; and its management has now passed into purely criminal hands; and its profits allow a degree of permanent organisation of crime that would not otherwise exist. This is the natural consequence of penalising what cannot be prevented.

As for our freedom of the written word, even that is not securely founded. The existing state of affairs rests on a series of Jury verdicts that reflect the more relaxed moral climate of the years since 1960. There is nothing to prevent future Juries from consenting to a fresh persecution. Also, the old laws of seditious and blasphemous libel remain in existence. The former has not been used by the authorities since 1948, and then unsuccessfully. But the latter, having been thought obsolete since 1922, was put to an ingenious use in 1978. I doubt if anyone who followed it in the newspapers will forget the case of *Whitehouse v Lemon & Gay News*.[31] In the absence of a clear law confirming the freedom of the press, what we have now is not so much freedom as permissiveness. What we have we hold not by right but on sufferance. That is undeniably bad.

Proposals for Reform

In the July of 1977, the Home Secretary in the Callaghan Government appointed a Committee on Obscenity and Film Censorship. Chaired by Bernard Williams, its task was "to review the laws concerning obscenity, indecency and violence in publications, displays and entertainments in England and Wales, except in the field of broadcasting [at the time under investigation by the Annan Committee], and to review the arrangements for film censorship in England and Wales; and to make recommendations."[32] The result was one of the clearest and most liberal

---

[31] See Geoffrey Robertson, senior defence counsel: "The Prosecutrix led prayer meetings in the corridors; the *Bible* replaced *Archbold* as the basic forensic reference; the jury (all of whom had taken the Christian oath) were supplied with Test-match scores by the judge—who later wrote a book congratulating himself, the deity and Mrs Whitehouse on the result. He confessed an 'extraordinarily unreal sensation' in writing and delivering his summing-up, which he attributed to his 'being guided by some superhuman inspiration'." (*ibid*, p. 211)

[32] *The Williams Report* was published in 1979 by HMSO as Cmnd. 7772. Its membership was: Bernard Williams, B. Hooberman, John Leonard,, Richard

state papers of modern times.

The Committee reviewed the existing law, and found it hopelessly vague and contradictory. It invited and examined evidence as to the corrupting effects of pornography. That submitted by the pro-censorship faction was rejected with well-merited contempt. Where not unsupported assertion, much of it was found to rest on an empirical base so narrow, so flimsy as to be laughable.[33] It concluded on the basis of the evidence available that no measurable harm could be ascribed to the influence of pornography. It did, however, bear in mind that the public display of certain material was deeply offensive to many members of the public; and that it was entirely legitimate to seek ways of preventing, or, at least, of minimising this offence. It also bore in mind the very reasonable need to protect children and young persons. It main legislative recommendations were as follows:

Matthews, David Robinson, Shiela Rothwell, A.W.B. Simpson. Anthony Storr, M.J. Taylor, John Tinsley, Polly Toynbee, J.G. Weightman, V.A. White. I am currently quoting from para 1.1.

[33] See, for example, the evidence submitted by one Dr Court, reviewed at para 6.31: "First, in relation to the availability of pornography in England and Wales, it needs to be said that no information exists to provide any kind of index. In the papers submitted to us, Dr Court did not attempt to provide such information. He does however treat Britain as a 'liberal' country in which the detrimental effects of pornography are to be seen, and he identifies two times at which, he suggests, pornography became increasingly available—first with a change in the law introduced by the Obscene Publications Act of 1964, and subsequently following the impetus of the American Commission Report on Pornography in 1970. Dr Court offers nothing to substantiate his statement and we find his explanation of the significance of these two dates less than convincing. As we have explained earlier, the Obscene Publications Act 1964 was a minor measure designed to strengthen the existing law by plugging two loopholes which had been found in the Act of five years previously. Dr Court cites as the only authority for his suggestion that pornography became more available after the enactment of the 1964 Act an article by Mr Ronald Butt on 5 February 1976 which attacked what Mr Butt then found to be the ineffectiveness of the law in controlling pornography. Mr Butt argued that the intention of the 1959 and 1964 Acts had been systematically destroyed over the years by the exploitation of their letter, but nothing in his article supports the idea that the 1964 Act opened the way to the greater availability of pornography. Nor do we know of any authority for the suggestion that pornography became more freely available here after 1970 as a result of the influence of the Report of the US Commission. It seems to us that the choice of the years 1964 and 1970 as crucial in the increasing availability of pornography is purely arbitrary."

- That all the existing laws relating to pornography should be repealed and replaced with a single comprehensive statute;
- That there should be no restrictions or prohibitions on the printed word;
- That, in order to prevent the giving of undue offence and to protect children and young persons, certain kinds of material should be restricted to sale only in special, clearly distinguished premises, that would be forbidden to mount offensive displays in their windows;
- That, in distinguishing this class of material, terms such as "obscene" and "indecent" and "deprave and corrupt" should be abandoned as both vague and obsolete;
- That in their place should be substituted the following formula: that the matter to be restricted should be that "which, not consisting of the written word, is such that its unrestricted availability is offensive to reasonable people by reason of the manner in which it portrays, deals with or relates to violence, cruelty or horror, or sexual, faecal or urinary functions, or genital organs";[34]
- That a smaller class of material should be entirely prohibited—this to "consist of material whose production appears to the court to have involved the exploitation for sexual purposes of any person, where either
- that person appears from the evidence as a whole to have been at the relevant time under the age of sixteen, or
- the material gives reason to believe that actual physical harm was inflicted on that person";[35]
- That the existing censorship of films should be abolished and a new one established to give effect to the reforms suggested above.

The effects of such a statute would be wholly beneficial. A vast burden of censorship would be lifted without shocking a mass of prejudice. Those who wanted pornography would be able to go into any special shop and find it as freely available there as almost anywhere in the world. Others would be able to go into their local newsagent, and never again be reminded that there were coloured photographs to be had of naked

---

[34] *Ibid*, para 9.36.

[35] *Ibid*, para 10.6.

Freedom of Speech in England

men and women. The authorities would have their efforts confined to the seeking out and destruction of material that comprised perhaps less than a hundredth part of the market in pornography, and the suppression of which would be warmly applauded by nearly everyone. Corruption would cease. The mafias would go bankrupt. The Police and courts would have more time to deal with crimes against life and property. The only objectors would be Mary Whitehouse and her followers—for whom the offence lies not in the sight but in the mere availability of pornography—and a few paedophile voyeurs.

The Conservative Record: Text and Pictures

But the Thatcher Government, which came to power almost immediately after publication of the Williams Report, did little to bring about its suggested reforms. It did implement those that, by themselves, tended to further control. There was the Indecent Displays (Control) Act 1981—brought in by Tim Sainsbury, but given Government support. This obliged sex shops to black out their windows, to prevent access to young persons, and to warn all other customers of what lay behind the blackened windows. There was a provision in the Local Government (Miscellaneous Provisions) Act 1982. This empowered local authorities to license sex shops and similar premises. The effect of this was to allow total suppression in some areas, where Councils just would not grant licences. Where there was not suppression, there was often tight restriction. Of course, not demand, but only competition, was reduced; and the remaining shops were able to profit enormously from the closure of their rivals.

These Acts were a mild indication of what was to come. I blush as a Conservative to relate them. Yet, though I blush, I must relate them even so.

The Customs and Excise take over

According to section 42 of the Customs Consolidation Act 1876

> [t]he goods enumerated and described in the following table of prohibitions and restrictions inward are hereby prohibited to be imported or brought into the United Kingdom, save as hereby excepted.

All that now remain in this table are

> indecent or obscene prints, paintings, photographs, books, cards lithographic or other engravings, or any other indecent or obscene articles.

This section gives the Customs and Excise a wider power over what we may read or look at or use than the Police enjoy. The Police are obliged to proceed under the Obscene Publications Act 1959, and must convince a Jury that the article in question has a tendency to "deprave or corrupt." The Customs and Excise need only persuade a Magistrate that it falls into the looser category of what is "indecent or obscene." They are able, moreover, to prosecute anyone who deals with the article after its importation. In consequence, in many questions involving allegedly pornographic material, the authorities gave up seeking enforcement of the 1959 Act in favour of the 1876 Act.

In 1982, a company called Conegate tried to import into this country from West Germany a number of inflatable rubber dolls. These when inflated became life-size replicas of a woman's body, complete with three orifices. They were seized by the Customs and Excise as "indecent or obscene articles." The seizure was upheld in the condemnation proceedings before the Magistrates and on appeal to the Crown Court. But Conegate appealed next to the High Court, claiming that the seizure contravened Articles 30 and 36 of the Treaty of Rome.

Since 1973, our country has been a member of the European Economic Community. This is not merely a free trade organisation, but also an embryonic superstate. Its present final objective appears to be the subjugation of the United Kingdom to the status of an outlying province of a united Europe. Aided and abetted by certain misguided Britons, Jacques Delors may well achieve what Hitler and Napoleon, and every other foreign leader since the Emperor Claudius, failed to achieve. Already, our own laws have yielded priority to European law in our courts. Already, we can be made subject to laws that our own Parliament has not made, and to which it might take the strongest exception.

The great majority of Community decisions binding on us have been grossly illiberal. In 1989, for example, the Council of Ministers decided to ban the sale within the Community of any cigarette with a tar content of more than 15mg.[36] To come into effect from the end of 1992, this ban will prevent the sale of Senior Service, Capstan, Gold Flake and many other fine and historic brands. Again, the Germans have for several years

---

[36] *The Daily Telegraph*, London, 14th November 1989. I do not mention this restraint above, since it was objected to by the British Government—though not, I must confess, on the grounds that it was an unwarranted interference with our rights; but only on the grounds that such decisions are made more appropriately by the national governments than by the central institutions of the Community.

been pressing for a Community law against Sunday trading more restrictive than any that has ever existed in English law, and that no British government could by itself hope to soften.[37] These are laws that should not be made nationally, let alone by the central institutions of the Community. they, and hundreds and thousands of others no less objectionable have done much to weaken the regard in which the Community ought to be held by liberals. But the European Court is able not merely to load us with unwanted restrictions, but also to free us from the oppressions of our own government.

Article 36 of the Treaty of Rome allows the placing of restrictions on imports for the sake or preserving "public morality, public policy or public security." It does not, however, allow restrictions to "constitute a means of arbitrary discrimination or a disguised restriction on trade between Member States." It was claimed for Conegate that since there was no prohibition of the manufacture and sale of inflatable dolls in the United Kingdom, there ought to be none of their importation from elsewhere in the Community. To allow otherwise was to allow an "arbitrary discrimination or a disguised restriction on trade between Member States." The High Court referred the matter to the European Court, which found for Conegate.[38] The dolls were returned, and remain freely available.

In itself an important case, this immediately had a wider effect than on the right to import aids to masturbation. Conegate had the money to mount a long and expensive appeal for its right to do business. But its victory established a principle that automatically governed all similar cases. In 1985, thirty seven customs officials, evidently having nothing better to do, entered into Gay's the Word, a small bookshop in Bloomsbury that imports literature by and about homosexuals. This entry—codenamed "Operation Tiger"—resulted in the seizure of books by Oscar Wilde, Gore Vidal and Christopher Isherwood among others. Seventy of these books were selected for prosecution under the 1876 Act. It was beside the point that many of them had been openly on sale here for generations; that they had been freely available even under our old obscenity laws. All that mattered was that they had been imported and

---

[37] *The Daily Telegraph*, London, 29th September 1990.

[38] *Conegate v Commissioners of Customs and Excise* (No 121/85) Queen's Bench (1987) 254.

might therefore be eased into the category of the "obscene or indecent." The proprietors of the bookshop if found guilty faced sentences of up to two years in prison. The prosecution was dropped as soon as the Conegate decision was announced.

Our authorities have thus been restricted in their use of the 1876 Act. Formally, they need only liberalise imports from within the Community. But it would be impracticable to apply different tests to imports from different parts of the world. Even if they did, the American suppliers would simply reroute their goods through Holland or Germany. The Customs and Excise have duly been ordered to apply the more liberal test regardless of the exporting country. The European Court has done more for the cause of liberty in this respect than the Thatcher Government had the least inclination to do. The Government had, indeed, sanctioned the prosecutions, even if it had not actively directed them.

The Conservative Record: The Electronic Media

I have not so far mentioned television and video. They are both comparatively recent developments, and their legal treatment is largely separate from that of the other media. The Williams Committee considered neither. Its neglect of the former was required by its terms of reference. Its neglect of the latter cannot be explained unless we conclude that its members were blind to the revolution taking place even while its members were deliberating. Both are supremely important. They are already our prime form of mass communication, and their primacy seems to be assured well into the next century.

Compared with the cinema, the television screen appears a very feeble thing. Anyone who has seen *Gone With the Wind* at the cinema, and then broken in halves on the television, will understand what I mean. For sheer overwhelming impact, there is no comparison. But television more than compensates by its ubiquity. In many households, it is on nearly the whole time. Its effect is magnified by repetition. In the cinema, except for a few adverts, we are shown a set programme that we have chosen in advance. At home, we sit back for the most part and watch what is beamed at us. Because of its special status, television is deemed peculiarly suited to State regulation.

There are three main arguments to justify this. First, there is the supposed need to maintain the "quality" of programmes. Unless something better is rammed down our throats, we are told, we shall give ourselves up wholly to trivia. This is a patronising argument, and a false one. In a free broadcasting market, people are shown what they want to

Freedom of Speech in England

watch. What they want to watch is determined by certain pre-existing standards of taste. Too much has been said about the supposed badness of American taste. I look instead at Australia, where broadcasting has been deregulated for some years. From there we have had *Anzacs*—to my mind the most powerful and authentic series ever screened about the Great War. It easily beat the historically inaccurate and melodramatic *The Monocled Mutineer* from the BBC Drama Department. From there we have *Neighbours*—for me quite simply the best soap on television. It shows attractive people in attractive situations. Its scripts are of a generally high standard. I recall one very funny episode in which Mrs Mengel was trying to ensnare someone into matrimony. In its tension and *dénouement*, it easily rivalled anything even in Sheridan. As for the quality of our own television, the BBC has spent far more of the Licence-payers' money on Terry Wogan and Bruce Forsyth than it ever has on Shakespeare.[39]

Second, there is the argument over political balance. Television programmes are not to give too one-sided a view about political matters. I need say nothing more about this than that this argument—and the controls imposed by the Broadcasting Acts and the BBC Charter—have enabled the suppression of unpopular or unwanted views. Whatever we think of unilateral nuclear disarmament—and it did not turn out to be necessary for avoiding war with the Soviets—I find it disgraceful that *The War Game* was kept off our screens for more than two decades by an essentially political censorship. If such a censorship were ever applied to the press, I have no doubt but there would be an explosion of outrage. Broadcasting may be special for the reasons given above. It is not that special.

Third, there is the argument over indecency. Now, here we come not only to the general case for control given above, but also to the protection of children. We can shut them out of the bookshops and cinemas and theatres. But television goes straight into the home. We can make the broadcasters show their more adult programmes after 9 PM. But many children either sit up late every night or have their own televisions. There is a danger that they will be able to watch whatever is shown at whatever

---

[39] To do him credit, Mr Wogan has been known to make an effort. Some time in 1988, he remarked on how well Sylvester Stallone was doing out of his films about the French poet Rimbaud. Unfortunately, the joke fell flat. It raised not a titter among the carefully selected studio audience.

The Case against Sex Censorship: A Conservative View

time. Parents can make their own rulings. But they are not always around to enforce them.

But this point touches on one of the central problems of a free society. There are two classes of persons among us. There are free adults and unfree children, and we must do what we can to maintain the distinction between them. There is no alternative to this. We could try abolishing the distinction altogether. We could lower the one class or raise the other. But this would not be advisable. Instead, we must do our best to find a balance between the need to maintain the freedom of adults and to protect the children. There is no completely obvious place where this balance can be found, and there is room here for legitimate disagreement. My own view is that, where television is concerned, we must devolve the question from the State to parents. We must let them decide what their children are to watch, and hope that they have the judgment to decide properly and the will to uphold their decisions. If they choose too unwisely, let them by all means be punished when the facts come to light. But, as with drinking and smoking, where similar problems arise, the first line of defence, on any Conservative view, must be the individual household.

I deplore the restrictive provisions of the Broadcasting Acts and the BBC Charter. But, since these were in place long before the first election of the Thatcher Government, and were only renewed by it, they fall outside my present enquiry. I note with approval the breaking of the duopoly with the establishment of Channel Four in 1982. I note with approval the projected breaking of the triopoly in the New Broadcasting Act. I fear the new regulatory powers given to the Commission headed by Lord Rees-Mogg, but have as yet no idea how they will be used. In any event, the introduction of satellite broadcasting may effectively have abolished the old regulations. It will be hard for domestic broadcasters. But, when viewers can watch whatever they like, beamed into their satellite dishes from outside the British Government's jurisdiction, it may no longer matter what any particular Statute will say.

It is a different matter with video tapes. Unless recordings are to be made from satellite broadcasts, or smuggled in—and at least the latter is illegal—these must be bought or hired in this country. They are amenable to regulation. In one respect, they are more powerful still than television. Not only do they flow from the screen, but they can also be stopped and rerun. They can be frozen. They can be run forwards or backwards in slow motion. Before long, it will be possible to enlarge specified areas of

Freedom of Speech in England

the screen. They are ideally suited to the closest attention—and not just by the critics. A film or a television programme may contain one graphic scene of violence or coercive sex, but may be balanced by the rest of the narrative of which it forms a necessary part. But a video tape can be run through and watched again and again for that one scene alone.

What About "Snuff Videos"?

At this point, I feel, a brief digression is in order. One of the more lurid claims made in favour of control is that there exists an active market in "snuff" videos—films in which real suffering, including death, is inflicted. I admit that such films may exist. They are technically possible. There is an audience that would delight in watching them. But common sense alone is enough to tell me that they are incredibly rare. With a few exceptions that can probably be counted on the fingers of one hand, the only snuff that any British citizen has ever seen is the kind that is bought in jars at 72, Charing Cross Road. Consider:

First, it is illegal to make, or be in any way involved in the distribution of, a snuff film. The crimes involved are only incidentally covered by the Obscene Publications Act. They are covered by the law of murder or the Offences against the Person Act 1861. The maximum penalty is not a fine or a fairly short spell in prison, or both, but imprisonment for life. Bearing in mind this risk, I doubt if any such film could be brought to market at any but the most prohibitive price. That market must be limited not only to those who find pleasure in watching unsimulated torments, but to those who can also afford to watch them.

Second, even if a competent crew could be persuaded to take part in the filming, unsimulated torments must be of a generally lower quality than simulated ones. At least since the 1920s, art has been more convincing than life. Imagine that you are making a snuff film. A safe location has been found—in itself, no easy matter. A child has been bought and is now suffering all the tortures of the damned. Half way through the shoot, it dies. Or, all goes as planned until the culminating moment of death. Then the camera is knocked over, or the lighting is wrong, or something else happens to spoil the shot. In an ordinary studio, the special effect can be recreated, and the scene can be refilmed. In this hypothetical studio, you must either find another victim and start over again, or be content with a botched effort. It really is both better and cheaper to hire a special effects crew.

This has been found to be the invariable practice of film makers—whatever publicity claims they may rely on. Not one snuff film has ever

The Case against Sex Censorship: A Conservative View

fallen into Police hands, in this country or in the United States. All that have been seized have turned out on investigation to be fakes. I quote one British distributor: "Nobody had heard of *Cannibal Holocaust* till I wrote to Mary Whitehouse complaining about it. Once she got in on the act I couldn't run off enough copies to meet demand."[40]

Then there was *Snuff*, perhaps the most successful fraud ever perpetrated in this market. Many of the tabloid newspapers still refer to it as though the truth were unknown. It was released in America in 1976 by one Alan Shackleton. He had bought a low-budget zombie horror film called *Slaughter* from a Latin American company. He spent about $5,000 on a surprise ending, and packaged it as "the film that could only have been made in South America—WHERE LIFE IS CHEAP!" "He not only hired protesters to picket cinemas, but paid actors to pose as FBI agents and interrogate members of the audience, demanding the identity of the cast and crew, whose names were purposely kept a secret."[41]

It may have been this film that Clodagh Corcoran had in mind when she claimed to have seen a snuff movie:

> I want to describe it to you in detail. But I can not, because my mind won't let me. What I can tell you is that on that night I watched a man participate in the act of sex with a woman, and during that act he plunged a large hunting knife into her stomach and cut her open from vagina to breast. He then withdrew the knife and stuck it into her left hand, removing the first three joints from her fingers, which fell from the bed. The woman's eyes remained open, she looked at the knife and said "Oh God, not me." It took her approximately three minutes to die. The camera was left running. The film was then canned and put on the commercial market as entertainment.[42]

There are certain problems with this description. Is Ms Corcoran describing a film that she saw in the cinema?—in which case the last sentence is redundant. Or is she describing what she saw during the alleged making of this film?—in which case she should have gone to the Police long before she sat down in front of her word processor. In any

---

[40] Quoted from a briefing paper shown me by David Botsford, whose company, Outlaw Films, is considering a series of documentaries on the pornography trade. I record my thanks.

[41] *Ibid.*

[42] Clodagh Corcoran, *Pornography: The New Terrorism*, Dublin, 1989—quoted Thompson and Annetts, *op. cit.*, p. 181.

event, she has never to my knowledge shown her copy of the film: at a press conference to discuss her book, she claimed that her video player was broken.

Most recently, there were the "Shropshire 15"—the consenting adults sentenced by Judge Rant QC for the hideous—though hitherto unknown—crime of beating each other up in the privacy of their own homes.[43] They had filmed some of their more adventurous exploits on video. The tapes were seized by the Police, who were at first convinced that they had stumbled on a snuff operation. They were almost sorry when the truth came out. Detective Superintendent Michael Hames, head of Scotland Yard's Obscene Publications Squad, had to content himself with the observation that "sadistic pornography was becoming more bizarre, more violent and more widespread. He issued a warning that it would eventually lead to a death being filmed."[44]

I repeat—I admit that snuff films may have been made, and that one or two of them may have been transferred from celluloid to video tape. But they must be unbelievably rare—and beyond the purse of anyone but some very decadent mafia bosses. They are certainly so rare that, for all the feverish searches of the past generation, not a single real example has ever been discovered by the authorities. If one ever does come to light, it certainly ought to be suppressed. Its makers and distributors ought to suffer the sternest consequences prescribed by law. All copies ought to be destroyed. That is my opinion. That is the opinion of almost everyone. There is a much larger—though, comparative to the whole, a limited—category of films that also ought, on the Williams criteria, to be

---

[43] For further information on this bizarre case, see Sean Gabb, *Sado-Masochism and the Law: Consent versus Paternalism,* Libertarian Alliance, 1991.

[44] *The Times*, London, 20th December, 1990. They were perhaps more than sorry. It has long been claimed by the Police that "participants in many of the ugly scenes have been drugged in order to withstand the brutality that is inflicted on them. They believe that, after filming, many of the players are secretly treated by doctors who may be part of the small group of 'porn entrepreneurs' providing the material for the black market." ("Hard-Core Porn Haul to be Shown to MPs," *The Daily Telegraph*, London, 16th September, 1990).

Note the mood of doubt or hypothesis in this claim. There is no proof that any of this happens, but the Police are inclined to believe that it does: and so they lobby for further laws—which they will then use, not against snuff makers, but against any club of consenting adults with a taste for sado-masochism and the ability to use a video camera.

prohibited. There is a still larger category that ought to be restricted in their distribution to adults only. The Williams Report is annoyingly silent where video tapes are concerned. But its prescriptions are easily applied to the new market. If they were so applied, there might be a few dozen films made unavailable, and several hundred more to be had only from those specialist shops dealing in other erotica. But, in its legislation here, the Thatcher Government chose to ignore the Williams Report both in letter and in spirit.

The Video Recordings Act

The current Obscene Publications Act, though dating from 1959, is sufficiently wide in its drafting to include video tapes. After a few months of legal ambiguity, it was held by the Court of Appeal that they were subject to prosecution in the same way as any other item that might be considered obscene. The one difference concerned what had to be taken into account by the Jury. Certain books and what was shown at the cinema might safely be presumed to be available for the most part only to adults. But videos were designed for home viewing; and it was pertinent to decide whether children might have access to them.[45] In 1983, a Jury convicted the distributors of *Nightmares in a Damaged Brain*. But the video revolution led to a fierce moral panic. There might already be a law in place. That law might already have been pronounced unnecessarily strict. But a supposed plague of video "nasties" was cried up in the press, and the usual sorts of politician began to demand a "tough new law."

At first, there was legal chaos. The Police began to raid video hire shops and confiscate as obscene films that had been granted certificates by the BBFC and had been freely shown in the cinemas. Then, pending legislation, the Attorney General issued a list of sixty films that would entail a prosecution if found for hire or sale. This quietened the Police and was greeted with relief by the trade. Those films listed nearly vanished from circulation. Almost no one pointed out the similarities of this list in principle with the famous *Index of Forbidden Literature* by which the Roman Catholic Church tried until the middle of the nineteenth century to keep its flock from knowing about the work of Copernicus, Bacon and Galileo. Almost no one pointed out the novelty of this list in English law. Some of the films condemned by it had been acquitted by Juries. Others were considered to be masterpieces.

---

[45] *Attorney-General's Reference*, No 5 of 1980 [1980], All England Reports, 816.

Freedom of Speech in England

So that these 60 films could be legally suppressed, the Video Recordings Act was passed in 1984. If the Attorney General's list was a legal novelty, this Act revived in full the principles of the Licensing Act that expired in 1695. Before then, all books, with a few exceptions, had to be submitted to a central agency for approval. Some were prohibited in full. Many were approved only after deletions or other alterations. It was an offence to publish without the required licence. After the Act expired, the doctrine of prior restraint was to vanish from these islands for the next 289 years. Then it reappeared.

The BBFC was finally recognised in law, the "C" sanitised from Censors to Classification. Its staff was increased from 12 to 50. It moved to larger premises. It acquired two Vice Presidents, both appointed by the Home Secretary. It now has the duty and the power to examine every item released on video, excepting a few of a scientific or educational nature, and to see whether it is fit for "viewing in the home," and if it is, for which age groups it is fit. Of those not judged fit it is to insist on the necessary alterations. Those judged altogether unfit are to be refused a licence. Anyone involved in the distribution of an unlicensed tape is liable to a fine not exceeding £20,000.

That the contents of any video tape have previously been on general release in the cinemas, or shown on television, does not at all imply that a licence will be granted, or that cuts will not be required. Nor does it matter whether they are for hire or sale only in sex shops. The test, it must be emphasised, is not obscenity, nor any of the regulations that govern broadcasting. The test is suitability for "viewing in the home." It may be, as Geoffrey Robertson argues,[46] that this imposes a less severe censorship than was at the time feared or promised. The BBFC is required, on granting a licence, to indicate for which age group a film is suitable. Parliament might, had it wished, have insisted that all videos be suitable for family viewing. It did not. Instead, it created a system of age classification. Therefore, it left room for parental responsibility. It is left to parents to keep their children away from material classified as suitable for adults only. On this view, no statutory justification exists for demanding cuts from adult material save in those cases where a prosecution might be expected under the Obscene Publications Act or some other law.

---

[46] *Op. cit.*, p. 225.

The Case against Sex Censorship: A Conservative View

This view, however, is not taken by the BBFC itself. Its Guidelines on Violence state that

> where horror material is concerned, we have exercised a restraining hand on the explicitness of gory imagery because of our awareness that children and younger teenagers may be particularly tempted to watch such material.[47]

Accordingly, it has become an absurdly repressive body where the portrayal of violence is concerned. Its victims have not been confined to the cheaper and nastier end of the market. It demanded four minutes of cuts from Hitchcock's *Frenzy*—a film that had twice been already shown unexpurgated on television. It refused a licence altogether to *Death Wish*—a film that has been shown several times on television. Five seconds were cut from the Douglas Fairbanks version of *The Thief of Baghdad*. Twenty four seconds were cut from something called *Nikki, Wild Dog of the North*.

Not surprisingly, it is also absurdly repressive where the portrayal of sex is concerned. In 1989, a short film about Saint Theresa of Avila was submitted for classification. Visions of Ecstasy had no dialogue, but what it showed was somewhat controversial. In the first section, a heavily made-up Theresa stabs herself with a large nail and smears the blood over her body and her habit, which becomes disarranged. The accompanying note explains that this represents her religious longings. Next, a scantily-dressed woman appears and embraces Theresa. This, according to the note, is her unconscious self. After some fondling of each other, the two come across the body of the crucified Christ. He is not wearing many clothes. The ladies turn their attention to him.

This was refused a licence on account of its alleged blasphemy. It was refused on the advice of the BBFC's lawyers. There was no trial. Instead, the censors decided, following all their customs, old and new, to play safe. As we all ought by now to realise, the modern law of blasphemy has no existence except as an adjunct to the law of obscenity. The maker of the film might have safely made an epic of simple blasphemy. He might have reviled God as a Lord High Bogeyman, and Christ as a Pauline fake. He might have raised all those embarrassing questions about the chronology of Abraham's father. He might, in short, have repeated all the arguments that have contributed to the decline of Christianity since 1700, and suffered no legal consequence whatever. But

---

[47] Ibid.

Freedom of Speech in England

he mixed his blasphemy with sex, and had his film prohibited. Even the Obscene Publications Act would not have touched him. But there is another law in reserve for such cases—a law that dare not speak its real purpose, which is to strike at the unwary pornographer.

The Video Recordings Act is bad in itself. It is an attack on freedom of speech and on our more general freedom to do as we please without harming others. But there are attendant circumstances that make it worse than that. A film may be granted a licence by the BBFC. Its distributors may advertise that fact on the case and in the tape's first few seconds. It can still be seized by the Police and condemned as obscene by the courts. The distributors are placed not in double, nor even in treble, jeopardy by the law. They are placed in quadruple jeopardy. If they release a film on video tape, they must apply for a licence. If they obtain a licence, they must still avoid a prosecution for obscenity. If they avoid that, they may, where relevant, be liable to a prosecution for blasphemy. If they avoid that, but the video tapes are imported, already recorded, they must avoid having the tapes seized as obscene or indecent articles. I am confident that no other country in the civilised world allows its laws to bear so heavily yet so vaguely.

Added to these uncertain costs of bringing video tapes to market is the more certain cost of having them licensed. The BBFC is financed not by the taxpayer, but by the fees charged on every film examined. The current charge is calculated at just under £5 per minute of running time. The total cost has kept many silent and foreign and other minority interest films from being released on video.

Conclusion

I repeat—this campaign will not be fast or easy. So far as its immediate purpose is to change thinking within the Conservative party, it may not even be successful. The final purpose, which is to bring about a reform of the law, will be achieved—though, again, not necessarily by us. For the completion of the Single European Market in 1993 may force on our authorities some faint glimmer of common sense. Then again, it may not. According to the 1992 Manifesto,

> British domestic controls on pornography will remain in place even after the completion of the single European market.[48]

---

[48] Manifesto, *op, cit,*. p. 31.

The Case against Sex Censorship: A Conservative View

But this is perhaps more promise than intention. The Ministers will struggle. They will complain in Brussels, whining about "subsidiarity." They will listen attentively to Mrs Mary Whitehouse. But they will finally have to bring our own censorship laws into line with those of our more liberal Community partners. I contemplate this with a keen sense of humiliation. Once more, we shall have been made to do the right thing by the wrong body. But, considering how badly the Thatcher and Major Governments have handled this matter, I must look forward to foreign pressure as a great, if ambiguous, benefit.

In the meantime, however, it is worth campaigning—to try to change thinking within the Conservative Party; and to try to ensure that such liberalisation as may eventually be dictated from Brussels either will not be necessary, or will only complete the victory of an essentially domestic campaign.

OBITUARY,
DAVID ALEC WEBB (2012)[49]

David Alec Webb, wit, raconteur, well-known actor on stage, screen and television, and tireless—and ultimately successful—opponent of the laws against pornography, died on the 30th June this year, at the age of 81.

The son of a car worker, he was born in Luton in 1931. He attended Luton Grammar School, where he did well academically and became Head Boy. After national service in the Army Education Corps, where he became a sergeant, he got a scholarship to the Royal Academy of Dramatic Arts (RADA). From here, he embarked on a long and successful career that began on the West End stage, but soon migrated to television. He was a prominent character in the early days of *Coronation Street*. Worried about the dangers of typecasting, he soon moved on, and, between the 1960s and the beginning of the present century, made well over 700 appearances in television programmes. These included *Upstairs, Downstairs*, *Randall and Hopkirk (Deceased)*, *Tales of the Unexpected*, *Doctor Who*, and *The Avengers*. He also found time for the cinema, appearing in, among much else, *The Battle of Britain*. In a profession which, notoriously, has an unemployment rate of eighty per cent, he was never out of work.

He was at one point so committed to television, and so prolific, that he was mocked by some of his RADA friends as a "Telly Tart." His response was a magisterial wave of the arm and the explanation: "On the telly, dear boy, you don't have to get it right first time, and the repeat fees mean you'll never run out of gin." He was right. Even today, it is an

---

[49] This obituary was commissioned by *The Independent* newspaper in July 2012. Sadly, that month and the next saw the death of just about everyone else who could be compared to David, but was more famous—Gore Vidal and Eric Sykes, for example. Publication was delayed again and again, until it was no longer relevant. The obituary was eventually published in *The Libertarian Enterprise*, 23rd September 2012. My thanks to L. Neil Smith for permission to republish here.

Obituary, David Alec Webb

unusual week on ITV3 when David Webb is not seen and credited in one of its many repeats from the golden age of British television.

Popular, despite his success, in a profession somewhat given to jealousy, David was elected to the Council of Equity, the actors' trade union. Among his wide circle of close and longstanding friends was the comedian Frankie Howerd, whose lover he was for several years.

As well as an actor, though, David was also an outspoken libertarian; and it may be for the impact he had as a libertarian on law and policy in England that he will be best remembered. In 1976, he founded the National Council for the Reform of the Obscene Publications Acts (NCROPA), and began his long campaign against the prudes and censors of every political and religious complexion.

In those days, the laws against pornography were, in their principle and intent, very clear. For those on the inside—which included David—who had the right friends, or knew the right officers in the Metropolitan Police, there were no restrictions. For everyone else, it was "No Sex, Please: We're British." Pornography was defined as anything a jury could be nagged into agreeing had a tendency to "deprave and corrupt." This meant, for example, no open crotch shots for women, and no "stiffies" for men. On this latter, judges and learned counsel could spend days, and even weeks, solemnly considering whether a particular male organ was naturally large, or was supported by a convenient length of tubular steel furniture, or was illegally tumescent. Against this unfairness and absurdity, David stated his own principle to anyone who would listen: "So long as it's by and for consenting adults, nothing should be forbidden."

David used the circle of friends and contacts he had made as an actor to ensure that NCROPA could not be ignored. He attracted public support from Clement Freud MP, and funding from the organised sex industry. For a quarter of a century, he lobbied the Government while trying to gain support in the media. He also engaged in direct litigation when he thought it useful to bring test cases into court. It was a long and often frustrating struggle. In those days, hypocrisy about sex was almost universal, and the leading politicians of all parties were united in their public condemnation of "filth." In 1978, he even earned a personal condemnation in a *Sun* editorial—just across, of course, from its page three photograph!

He faced all this with good humour tinged with contempt. Once in a studio discussion programme, someone accused him of promoting sexual

Freedom of Speech in England

violence against women. "Don't be silly!" he snapped. "I've been in more comedy than you've had haircuts." To the applause of the audience, he continued: "It's had no effect on the amount of laughter you see in the streets."

Of course, the condemnation was often only in public. In 1981, David led a delegation to see William Whitelaw, the Home Secretary of the day. Whitelaw was completely sympathetic in private. But he flatly insisted that he could never get reform of the "porn laws" through the Cabinet or through Parliament.

In 1983, David stood for Parliament as a freedom of expression candidate. With his characteristic boldness and lack of respect for the great, he stood in Finchley against Margaret Thatcher. The Prime Minister was not amused—it is even possible that David's challenge strengthened her determination to push through the Video Recordings Act the following year. While campaigning, though, he struck up a long and convivial friendship with Carol Thatcher, the Prime Minister's daughter.

Success in the campaign came unexpectedly but all at once. Though happy to fund him, David's supporters in the sex industry had always been careful to avoid open challenge to the law. Then, in 2000, he managed to procure a commercial video which was rejected by the British Board of Film Classification (BBFC). David pushed the makers into appealing to the Video Appeal Committee—a body set up to comply with the Human Rights Act 1997. The VAC passed the video. The BBFC then appealed into the High Court. Its argument was that it was protecting a "vulnerable minority" which might be unbalanced by exposure to explicit material. The High Court ruled this "disproportionate" under the European Convention on Human Rights. The judgment was so strongly worded that the BBFC had no choice but to cave in and liberalise its guidelines defining obscenity.

One of the benefits of this judgment was that the Customs and Excise and the various police forces in England and Wales adopted these new guidelines for themselves, thereby giving up on their own, often far stricter, definitions of obscenity. It was a settlement of the issue that suited all parties. The increasingly ridiculous and—because of the Internet—increasingly unenforceable censorship of sexual expression largely fell to the ground. At the same time, no elected politician had to run the gauntlet of *Daily Mail* and pressure group disapproval. The changes were quietly accepted. In this respect, while the Blair

Government cannot be regarded as friendly to civil liberties, England became a slightly freer country.

In his later years, David was often told that his campaign had been a waste of time—that the Internet had done more to liberalise the law than all his campaigning. His reply was a shrug and: "By 1967, too many of us were openly buggering each other for the law to be strictly enforced. Does that mean campaigning for that year's Sexual Offences Bill was a waste of time? Just because a law is unenforceable doesn't mean it can't be rolled out now and again to destroy a few lives. I did my bit to make this country a better place. I'm not disappointed by the result."

In private life, David was a grand, convivial character, who loved good company, good food, good drink, and classical music. He was diagnosed with pancreatic cancer early in 2012, and its progress was so rapid that he had no time to stop being the man his friends had all known and loved. He faced his end with the equanimity of a true follower of Epicurus. He died peacefully and in his sleep at Trinity Hospice in Clapham. He was 81. His funeral was at Mortlake Crematorium on the 17th July 2012. As might be expected, it was a diverse and not wholly joyless event.

He is survived by his sister Pam and his goddaughter Nikki.

REFLECTIONS ON THE GARY GLITTER CASE (1999)[50]

Paul Gadd, performing under the name Gary Glitter, was a very popular British singer in the early to middle 1970s. Even as a child, I had no liking for rock music. But I did notice and like Gary Glitter. It was not for his songs, which were as unmemorable as all the others of his day. What made me notice him was the wild extravagance of his dress—all sequins and tight trousers—thrown carelessly over a figure that was always verging on the fat. What made me like him was the pleasant and self-deprecating manner in which he handled television interviews. He seemed surprised at his popularity, and even a little contemptuous of the public taste that had raised him so high.

I lost sight of him after about 1974, and gave him no more thought until I heard last year of his difficulties with the criminal law. Apparently, he had bought a computer from PC World, which is the largest computer retailer in the United Kingdom, had used this for a while, and then had taken it back to have its various faults put right. The repair engineer discovered a number of pornographic images on the hard disk and called the police. Mr Gadd was charged with possession of child pornography under the Protection of Children Act as amended in 1988 and 1994.[51]

---

[50] Published on *www.seangabb.co.uk* on the 14th November 1999.

[51] The law has been created as follows:

Section 1 of the Protection of Children Act 1978 reads:

It is an offence for a person—

(a) to take, or permit to be taken, any indecent photograph of a child (meaning in this Act a person under the age of 16); or (b) to distribute or show such indecent photographs; or (c) to have in his possession such indecent photographs, with a view to their being distributed or shown by himself or others; or (d) to publish or cause to be published any advertisement likely to be understood as conveying that the advertiser distributes or shows such indecent photographs, or intends to do so.

Reflections on the Gary Glitter Case

Sometime after this, a middle-aged woman came forward and accused Mr Gadd of having seduced her when she was fourteen and of having kept her as a "sex slave" for the next twelve years.

The case reached its end last Friday the 12th November [1999]. The Jury cleared Mr Gadd of all charges in connection with the middle-aged woman, but he had already pleaded guilty to the child pornography charges, and the Judge sentenced him to four months in prison. The news report on this I heard predicted that it meant the end of Gary Glitter. Bearing in mind the number of young and not so young women who danced and cheered in the public gallery and outside the court as the news of his partial acquittal, and his ability to survive all the changes of fashion in the past quarter century, I am not so sure. Gary Glitter will be banned

---

Section 160(1) of the Criminal Justice Act 1988 amends this Section by adding that

It is an offence for a person to have any indecent photograph of a child (meaning in this section a person under the age of 16) in his possession.

Section 84(2) of the Criminal Justice and Public Order Act 1994 further amends the 1978 Act as follows:

In section 1 (which penalises the taking and indecent photographs of children and related acts)—

(a) in paragraph (a) of subsection (1)

(i) after the word "taken" there shall be inserted the words "or to make", and the words following "child" shall be omitted;
(ii) after the word "photograph" there shall be inserted the words "or pseudo-photograph....

The wording of the other paragraphs of the 1978 and 1988 Acts is similarly changed to reflect the creation of the new offence.

Section 7(5) of the 1978 Act is amended to read as follows:

(6) "Child", subject to subsection (8), means a person under the age of 16.

(7) "Pseudo-photograph" means an image, whether made by computer-graphics or otherwise howsoever, which appears to be a photograph.

(8) If the impression conveyed by a pseudo-photograph is that the person shown is a child, the pseudo-photograph shall be treated for all purposes of this Act as showing a child and so shall a pseudo-photograph where the predominant impression conveyed is that the person shown is a child notwithstanding that some of the physical characteristics shown are those of an adult.

In this section the laws of Scotland and Ulster are also amended to the same effect.

Freedom of Speech in England

from every radio station in the English-speaking world, but his live concerts will never be less than standing room only.

Now what I find so interesting about this case is not the personality of Gary Glitter, but how it illustrates the best and the worst about the British system of justice. Let me begin with the middle-aged woman.

It is absurd that charges of seduction can be brought so long after the alleged event. I do not share Peter Tatchell's belief that the age of consent should be lowered to fourteen, and I do believe that adults who have sex with young people under a certain age should face criminal charges. But there surely ought to be a time limitation on bringing such charges. To let them be brought without any limitation is an abuse of justice. A child who complains immediately after an alleged assault should be listened to. An adult who complains twenty or thirty years after the event should be told to go away. I think it reasonable that anyone who spends so long brooding over what may have awful at the time, but which with the passing of years must have become decreasingly awful, should not be seen as a reliable witness. At the very best, dates and places and other facts become blurred in the memory of all parties. At worst, elaborate lies can be told against which there can be no easy defence. Indeed, though I am uncertain of the details in this particular case, I suspect that complaints of this kind are often brought by unsuccessful blackmailers.

The injustice is heightened by the anonymity guaranteed by law to the accuser. Someone who stood up in court three centuries ago and accused an old woman of cursing his sheep was known to the Jury and had his name reported in the newspapers and the court records of the day. The middle-aged woman who accused Mr Gadd was unknown to the Central London Jury who judged her evidence, and her name cannot be published anywhere. I do not know if she was lying. But the fact that no one will ever know her name must have been an incentive not to tell the truth. Except she still had to give her evidence in person, the procedure was borrowed straight from the Inquisition. This corruption of process is an achievement of the feminist movement, aided by politicians and civil servants who instinctively hate the old notion of equality before the law. The next step—already demanded, though not yet granted—is to reverse the burden of proof, so that the defence will need to prove innocence.

Then there is the partiality with which the law is applied. If ever accused of legal oppression and wasting taxpayers' money, the authorities will hide behind a wall of excuses about having had no choice but to prosecute. "The evidence was there," they will say. "There was a *prima*

Reflections on the Gary Glitter Case

facie case against Mr Gadd. It was our legal duty to prosecute and let a Jury decide." This is a lie. The authorities have almost unlimited discretion over what cases to drop and what to pursue. Look, for example, at a recent case in Lancashire. Eleven Asians were charged with the murder of a young white man. Just before the trial started, all the murder charges were dropped. This was not for want of evidence, but because "prosecution would not be in the public interest." It would not be in the public interest because it would mean letting the media report that some parts of this country are sliding into a low intensity civil war between different ethnic groups.[52]

Or look at the Mr Gadd's accuser. She had accepted money from *The News of the World* for her story, and had been promised another £25,000 if Mr Gadd was found guilty. Will she be charged with contempt of court and sent to prison for two years? I doubt it. Her example will be used to justify further censorship of the media, but she will never be punished under the known, ancient laws against what she did.

I turn now to the pictures found on Mr Gadd's computer. There is no certainty that these were of young persons under the age of sixteen. The police make it their habit to classify all pornographic images they find as of children, no matter how old the models actually appear to be. They then rely on threats of exposure in the newspapers and castration in prison to force a confession to something else. It may be that Mr Gadd held out too long. Or perhaps he really was guilty under the law. We shall never know, as he confessed to possession at the last minute, and the pictures were not shown in court. But let us assume that these pictures were of children. This being so, are there any credible reasons why *possessing* them should be illegal?

I will say here, for the avoidance of doubt, that, just as it is rightly against the law to have sex with children, so it is rightly against the law to produce images of children that are plainly sexual. It is also rightly illegal to distribute such images. Producers and distributors of child pornography should be sent to prison—after, of course, a fair trial.

---

[52] The case was reported BBC Radio 5's Drive programme on the 3rd November 1999. The interviewer was Peter Allen. Robert Henderson, who told me about the case, checked *The Daily Telegraph*, *The Times*, *The Guardian*, *The Independent*, *The Daily Express*, *The Daily Mail*, and *The Mirror*. Not one carried a single word about the story.

Freedom of Speech in England

This being said, I take the standard libertarian position that an act should be criminal only so far as it can be shown to have caused an identifiable individual harm that would be recognised as such by a reasonable person. Mr Gadd's taste in pornography may be ugly, and should certainly make people think less of him than they did. But what actual harm did he cause to identifiable individuals?

One answer is that if Mr Gadd had taken them himself, the pictures would be evidence of a crime as defined above. It would be the same if he had procured somebody else to take them. That would make him an accessory to a crime. By all means, let such acts be criminal, and let them be punished. But the crime here would not be *possession*: possession would be no more than *evidence* of a crime. In any event, there is no claim that he ever knew the models or the photographers. He appears simply to have downloaded them from the Internet.

Another answer is that looking at such pictures somehow encourages attacks on children. There is a vast literature on the alleged inflammatory nature of pornography, and I will not refer to it beyond saying that I have yet to be shown a causal connection between pornography of any kind and sexual violence. But I will observe that if Mr Gadd, as we are told, spent up to twelve hours a day downloading his pictures, he can have had little time for doing much else.

And I will observe that if possession of child pornography is to be banned because it might provoke attacks on children, possession of all pornography ought to be banned for the protection of everyone else. And once we have done this with pornography, we should extend the ban to most kinds of religious and political literature. I have no idea how many sexual murders there have been in the past five centuries, but I doubt if they amount to even a thousandth of one per cent of those committed for the greater glory of God or the welfare of the masses. To imprison Mr Gadd because he had some indecent pictures, and let others go for having copies of *The Bible* or *The Communist Manifesto,* is at the very least inconsistent.

An answer still less convincing is that, by downloading the pictures, he was somehow encouraging their production. This would be the case had he commissioned them. But I am not aware that he commissioned anything. So far as I am aware, he downloaded his pictures from various newsgroups and open access web sites. I once borrowed a book from my school library that had pictures of the Jack the Ripper victims. Was I thereby encouraging serial sex murder? I think not.

Again, I am not condoning any exploitation of children, and I will emphasise again that the sexual use of children should remain a crime. If I am emphasising this point, it is because I am aware of how easy it is for comments on this issue to be taken out of context and used to make false and scurrilous allegations. So here it is again: ***I am not in any sense arguing for a right of adults to use children for any sexual purpose.*** All I am asking is that the law should be confined to the protection of children.

The most likely use of this law is not to protect children, but to give the police unlimited power to destroy anyone they do not like by planting evidence. If a man is accused of murder, a body must be produced. If he is accused of even a "victimless crime" like selling drugs or pornography, some objective evidence must be produced in court—either witnesses or a paper trail showing payment of suppliers and laundering of the proceeds. But a law against possession of certain images makes it frighteningly easy to get convictions on the basis of planted evidence. Let the police "find" the wrong sort of image on someone's hard disk or among his books, and there is no need to prove how it got there.

And this is a point I would urge even on those who may disagree with the points I make above. The idea that our police are scrupulously honest is nowadays too absurd to need refuting. For the safety of everyone, and not just men like Paul Gadd, they must be required in any prosecution to produce objective evidence. I accept that the sexual use of children is an explosive issue. But it is by the unscrupulous use of explosive issues like this one that the practice of our old Common Law is being replaced by the practice of the Inquisition.

I did say that I would mention what is good about the British system of criminal justice. This is Trial by Jury. So long as twelve ordinary people have the unrestricted right to find someone not guilty even in the face of the evidence, we still live in a reasonably free country. The authorities in this country have turned democratic accountability into a joke, and can make whatever laws take their fancy. But the enforcement of these laws will always be partly restrained by the need to persuade a Jury that they should be enforced. I did not follow Mr Gadd's trial with close attention, but I am ready to believe that the Jury acquitted him of the charges brought before it partly because of the oppression involved in laying such charges so long after the alleged event and because of the evident unsoundness of the only prosecution witness.

Freedom of Speech in England

I will not say more about Trial by Jury, however, as it is on the way to abolition. The Government is about to bring in a Bill to limit the right to no more than a few hundred cases a year; and this last remnant will be swept away as soon as the Government introduces the *Corpus Juris*—that is, full harmonisation with European criminal law: no Trial by Jury, no *habeas corpus*, no presumption of innocence, no rule against double jeopardy, and so forth.

So here are my comments on the Gary Glitter case. I cannot say anything in his favour. Perhaps I should have said nothing at all. Nevertheless, he has been punished by a frightening law, and this should be looked at.

ON GOLLIWOGS, ONE-EYED SCOTTISH IDIOTS, AND SENDING POO THROUGH THE POST (2009)[53]

In England, one of those weeks has just ended that define an entire period. This is no consolation for those who have suffered, and who may yet suffer worse. But I have no doubt that it is worth describing what has happened and trying to explain what it means.

Let me begin with the facts.

First, it was reported on the 3rd February 2009 that Carol Thatcher, daughter of Margaret Thatcher, had been dismissed from her job as a BBC presenter for having called a black tennis player a golliwog. She did not say this on air, but during a private conversation. Even so, the BBC defended its decision on the grounds that any language of a "racist nature" was "wholly unacceptable."

Second, demands are rising at the moment for Jeremy Clarkson, another presenter at the BBC, to be dismissed for having called the Prime Minister a "one-eyed Scottish idiot who keeps telling us everything's fine." Various Scotch politicians and spokesmen for the blind let up an immediate chorus of horror that has resulted in a conditional apology from Mr Clarkson, but may not save his career.

Third, it was reported on the 2nd February 2009 that the comedian and Labour Party supporter Jo Brand was being investigated by the police for allegedly inciting criminal acts against her political opponents. While presenting a BBC television programme on the 16th January 2009, she rejoiced that the membership list of the British National Party had been stolen and published on the Internet. Her exact words were: "Hurrah! Now we know who to send the poo to."[54] The natural meaning of her words was that it would be a fine idea to look up members of this party and send excrement to them through the post. The British National Party

---

[53] Published on *www.seangabb.co.uk* on the 8th February 2009.

[54] News report, "Jo Brand's BNP joke reported to police," *The Daily* Telegraph, London, 2nd February 2009.

put in an immediate complaint, using the hate speech laws made during the past generation. According to a BBC spokesman, "We do not comment on police matters. However, we believe the audience would have understood the satirical nature of the remarks." [55] It is relevant to note that Mrs Brand was present when Carol Thatcher made her "golliwog" remarks, and may have had a hand in denouncing her.

Fourth, In *The Times* on the 6th February, someone called Matthew Syed wrote how personally oppressed he felt by words like "golliwog," and how good it was that "society" was taking a stand against them. Two pages later, someone called Frank Skinner[56] defended the employers in the north of England who prefer to employ foreigners on the grounds that foreigners are "better looking" and "less trouble." The possibility that he has broken one of our hate speech laws will probably never be considered.

This is a gathering of facts that occurred or were made public during one week. But if we relax the time limit, similar facts pour in beyond counting. There was, for example, the pillorying last month of one of the Queen's grandsons for calling someone a "Paki." [57] Or, to give myself as an example, there was my BBC debate of the 16th February 2004 with Yasmin Alibhai-Brown, an Asian immigrant who seems incapable of seeing any issue except in terms of white racism. During this debate, I asked her: "Yasmin, are you saying that the white majority in this country is so seething with hatred and discontent that it is only restrained by law from rising up and tearing all the ethnic minorities to pieces?" Her answer was "Yes." It is possible she did not understand my question. It is possible she would have clarified or retracted her answer had the debate been allowed to continue. Sadly for her, the BBC immediately switched off my microphone and threw me into the street. Mrs Brown was allowed to continue uninterrupted to till the end of the programme. The hundreds of complaints received by the BBC and the Commission for Racial

---

[55] James Millbank, "New BBC taste row as police probe Jonathan Ross stand-in Jo Brand's anti-BNP joke," *The Daily Mail*, London, 2nd February 2009.

[56] This reference has now disappeared behind the Murdoch Paywall. If you have paid to look over this, go here:

www.timesonline.co.uk/tol/comment/columnists/frank_skinner/article5671420.ece

[57] David Harrison and Jon Swaine, "Prince Harry's 'Paki' comments 'completely unacceptable', says David Cameron," *The Daily Telegraph*, London, 11th January 2009.

On Golliwogs and Other Things

Equality were all either ignored or dismissed with the assurance that nothing untoward had taken place in the studio. I accept that Mrs Brown might not have meant what she said. Had I made such a comment about Asians or blacks, however, I might have been facing a long stretch in prison.

But let me return to the most recent facts. The most obvious reason why these broadly similar incidents are being treated so differently is that Jo Brand and Frank Skinner are members of the new ruling class that formally took power in 1997. They can vilify their opponents as freely as Dr Goebbels did his. Any of the hate speech laws that might—objectively read—moderate their language will be regarded as nullities. The police had no choice but to investigate Mrs Brand for her alleged offence committed live on television before several million people. But they made it clear that no charges would result. According to a police spokesman, "The chances of this going further are very remote. The idea that the BNP are claiming they are the victim of a race offence is mildly amusing, to say the least."[58] It may be amusing. The statement itself is interesting, though, as a formal admission that law in this country now means whatever the executive finds convenient.

Carol Thatcher and Jeremy Clarkson are not members of the the ruling class. They have no such immunity. Mr Clarkson may get away with his act of hate speech because he is popular and clever, and because the main object of his contempt is only the Prime Minister. Miss Thatcher may not be allowed to get away with her act. She used a word that borders on the illegal. And she is the daughter of Margaret Thatcher. She is the daughter, that is, of the woman elected and re-elected three times on the promise that she would make the British State smaller and stop it from being made the vehicle for a totalitarian revolution by stealth. Of course, she broke her promises. She did nothing to stop the takeover of the state administration by politically correct totalitarians. But there was a while when the people who actually won the cultural revolution in this country thought they would lose. They looked at her rhetoric. They noted the millions of votes she piled up in her second and third general elections. And they trembled. As said, they won. Mrs Thatcher herself is too old to suffer more than endless blackening at the hands of the victors who now comprise the ruling class. But they still tremble at the thought of how her

---

[58] James Millbank, "New BBC taste row as police probe Jonathan Ross stand-in Jo Brand's anti-BNP joke," *The Daily Mail*, London, 2nd February 2009.

shadow darkened their 1980s. And if they can do nothing to her now, her daughter can be ruined, and that will now be tried with every chance of success.

It might be argued that what Miss Thatcher and Mr Clarkson said was offensive, and that they are in trouble because we have a much greater regard for politeness than used to be the case. Perhaps it is offensive to say that a black man looks like a golliwog. Perhaps it is offensive to imply that Scotchmen are idiots or that people with defective sight also have defective judgement. It might be. But it might also be offensive to millions of people that the BBC—which is funded by a compulsory levy on everyone who can receive television signals—broadcasts a continual stream of nudity and obscene language; and that it pays the biggest salary in its history to Jonathan Ross, whose only public talent is for foul-mouthed buffoonery. The British ruling class—especially through the BBC, its main propaganda outreach—has a highly selective view of what is offensive.

And it is worth replying that the alleged offensiveness of the statements is minimal. Let us forget about golliwogs and implied sneers at the blind. Let us take the word "nigger." Now, this has not been a word admitted in polite company in England since about the end of the eighteenth century. Anyone who does use the word shows himself a person of low breeding. Whatever its origins, its use for centuries has been as an insult to black people. Any reasonable black man, therefore, called a nigger, has cause to take offence.

This being said, only moderate offence can be reasonable. Anyone who runs about, wailing that he has been hurt by a word as if it were a stick taken to his back, and calling for laws and social ostracism to punish the speaker, is a fool or a villain. And I can think of few other epithets that a reasonable person would greet with more than a raised eyebrow—"poof," "paki," "papist," "mohammedan," "chinkie" and the like. Anyone who finds these words at the very worst annoying should grow up. We can be quite sure that most of the Asian languages now spoken in this country contain some very unflattering words to describe the English—for example, *goreh*, *gweilo*, and so forth. There is no pressure, internal or external, for these to be dropped. And we know that there are any number of organisations set up by and for non-whites in this country from which the English are barred—for example, the National Black Police Association.

On Golliwogs and Other Things

However, the highly selective use of speech codes and hate speech laws has nothing really to do with politeness. It is about power. The British ruling class may talk the language of love and diversity and inclusiveness. What it obviously wants is the unlimited power to plunder and enslave us, while scaring us into the appearance of gratitude for our dispossession. Because the tyrannised are always the majority in a tyranny, they must be somehow prevented from combining. The soviet socialists and the national socialists kept control by the arbitrary arrest and torture or murder of suspected opponents. That is not presently acceptable in England or in the English world. Control here is kept by defining all opposition as "hatred"—and by defining all acts or attitudes that might enable opposition as "hatred."

I am the Director of the Libertarian Alliance. Not surprisingly, my own opposition to the rising tide of despotism is grounded on a belief in individual rights. I may occasionally talk about my ancestral rights as an Englishman, or about how my ancestors fought and died so I could enjoy some now threatened right. I may sometimes half-believe my rhetoric. Ultimately, though, I believe that people have—or should be regarded as having—rights to life, liberty and property by virtue of their human status. Anything else I say really is just a rhetorical device. This is not the case with most other people. For them, opposing the encroachments of a ruling class is grounded on collective identity—"*they* can't do that to *us*." Now, this sense of collective identity may derive from common religion, common loyalty, common culture, but most often and most powerfully—though these other sources may also be important—from perceived commonality of blood.

This collective identity is not something that is seen at times of emergency, but otherwise is in abeyance. It is important in times of emergency so far as it is always present. People work together when they must because, at all other times, they have a mass of shared rituals and understandings that hold them together. These shared things often define a people in terms of their distinctness from others. Jokes beginning "There was an Englishman, an Irishman and a Scotchman" or "What do you call a Frenchman who...?" are part of what reinforces an English identity. So too are comments and gestures and assumptions that assert the superiority of the English over other peoples. To change my focus for a moment, take the phrase *Goyishe Kopf*—Gentile brains! This is what some Jews say when they do something stupid. It can be taken as expressing hatred and contempt of non-Jews. More reasonably, it is one of those comments that reinforce the Jewish identity.

What Carol Thatcher said was part of this reminding of identity. Her exact words, so far as I can tell, were: "You also have to consider the frogs. You know, that froggy golliwog guy." The meaning she was trying to convey was: "let us consider how quaint and absurd outsiders are. Is it not nice that we are members of the same group, and that we are so clever and so beautiful?" I am not saying that I approve of what she actually said. Indeed, she would have done better for herself and the English in general had she kept her mouth shut. Calling someone "froggy" is neither here nor there. Calling him a "golliwog" is moderately hurtful. Saying this on BBC premises, and in front of people like Jo Brand, shows that Miss Thatcher is stupid or that she was drunk. Her words, as reported, do less to reinforce English identity than make the whole thing an embarrassment.

However—her name always aside—she is being punished not because her words were crass, but because they fell into the category of actions that must at all times be discouraged. Powerful or crass to the point of embarrassment, nothing must be tolerated that might tend to promote an English identity. I say an *English* identity. The rule does not apply to Scotch or Welsh or Irish nationalism. These are not regarded as a danger to the ruling class project of total enslavement. They are controllable by subsidy. More usefully, they are anti-English. The various ethnic nationalisms and Islamic identities are likewise allowed or encouraged. They are not perceived as a danger to the ruling class project of total domination, and may be used against the English. It is English identity that must at all costs be repressed. The English are still the largest national group in these islands, and will remain so at least until 2040, when there may be a non-white majority all through the United Kingdom. English national ways are the raw material from which every liberal doctrine has been refined. The English are an unpleasantly violent nation when pushed too far.

This explains why words and expressions are defined almost at random as "hatred," and why names of groups and places keep changing almost at random. The purpose is not to protect various minority groups from being hurt—though clever members of these groups may take advantage of the protections. The real purpose is to hobble all expression of English identity. It is to make the words and phrases that come most readily to mind unusable, or usable only with clarifications and pre-emptive cringes that rob them of all power to express protest. Or it is to force people to consult their opponents on what words are currently acceptable—and whoever is allowed to control the terms of debate is likely to win the debate.

And look how easily it can be done. Also during the past week, we have seen working class demonstrations in the north of England against the employment of foreign workers. "British jobs for British workers" they have been chanting. A few raised eyebrows and warnings from Peter Mandelson about the "politics of xenophobia," and the trade unions have straightaway sold out their members and are preparing to bully them back to work. Better that trade union members scrabble to work for a pound an hour, or whatever, than that they should be suffered to use words like "Eyeties" or "Dagoes."

I should end by suggesting what can be done to counter this strategy. I suppose the answer is not to behave like Carol Thatcher. We must accept that certain words and phrases have been demonised beyond defence. Some of them are indefensible. These must be dropped. Others that are just about permissible—Scotchman, for example—should be used and defended on all occasions. We should also bear in mind that political correctness is not about protecting the weak but disarming the potentially strong, and it must be made clear to the ruling class that its management of language has been noticed and understood and rejected. A strategy of apparently casual offence, followed by partial and unconvincing apology—of the sort that we may have seen from Jeremy Clarkson—may also be appropriate.

Another strategy worth considering is the one adopted by the British National Party. In a free country, Jo Brand would be at perfect liberty to incite criminal acts against unnamed and reasonably unidentifiable people. But we do not live in a free country. There is a mass of laws that criminalise speech that was legal even a few years ago. The response to this is to invoke the laws against those who called for them. As said, people like Jo Brand and Yasmin Alibhai Brown are unlikely ever to be prosecuted for crimes of hate speech. But the authorities will occasionally be forced to go through the motions of investigating, and this can be made a form of harassment amounting to revenge. Otherwise, it is useful to establish beyond doubt that the laws are not intended to be enforced according to their apparently universal wording.

Freedom of Speech in England

There is much else to be said. But I suppose the most important thing is not to behave like Carol Thatcher. It will be unfair if she is broken by her words. But if you stick your head into a lion's mouth, you cannot really complain when you feel the teeth closing round your neck.

All told, this has been an interesting week. Understood rightly, it may turn out to have been a most productive week.

Yasmin Alibhai-Brown and Humour: No Laughing Matter (2010)[59]

I was called a few minutes ago by LBC, a commercial radio station that broadcasts within the London area. The researcher explained the biggest news story of the day and asked me for a comment. The story is that one Gareth Compton, who is a Conservative representative on Birmingham City Council, had made a joke on Twitter about the Moslem journalist Yasmin Alibhai-Brown. He said: "Can someone please stone Yasmin Alibhai-Brown to death? I shan't tell Amnesty if you don't. It would be a blessing, really." As soon as she heard about this, Mrs Alibhai-Brown announced that she would call the police and have the man charged with incitement to murder. But somebody else had already done so. Mr Compton was arrested, and then released on bail.

I made my comments immediately after hearing about the story, and they are rather scathing. However, I have now checked the news, and everyone else seems to be taking the matter very seriously. Mrs Alibhai-Brown is leading the hunt. "A politician validates the many people who do threaten columnists like me," she told Sky News[60]..." what you're saying is 'it's ok to hate so much that you kill a journalist and a writer'." A spokesman for the Conservative Party said that Mr Compton's language was "unacceptable," and that he had been suspended from the Party while he was investigated. A spokeswoman for Birmingham City Council added: "Any written complaints will be formally considered by the council standards committee to determine if any investigation should be held.... The committee will also be mindful of any criminal investigations concluded by the police."

---

[59] First Published on *www.seangabb.co*.uk on the 11th November 2010.

[60] news.sky.com/skynews/Home/Politics/Toy-Councillor-Gareth-Compton-Arrested-Over-Tweet-Calling-For-Yasmin-Alibhai-Brown-To-Be-Stoned/Article/201011215800467?lpos=Politics_Second_UK_News_Article_Teaser_Region_7&lid=ARTICLE_15800467_Toy_Councillor_Gareth_Compton_Arrested_Over_Tweet_Calling_For_Yasmin_Alibhai-Brown_To_Be_Stoned

Freedom of Speech in England

Mr Compton has now deleted his tweet and apologised for the remark, calling it "an ill-conceived attempt at humour."

It is difficult to know where to begin a written commentary on this matter. I suppose the right beginning is to take note of the English contempt of court laws. The news report I read does not say if Mr Compton had been charged with an offence. But he may yet be charged, and, once charges are laid, no one is allowed to make any comment that may prejudice his trial. And so I will not discuss whether Mr Compton did publish the words in question. Nor will I discuss whether publishing them is illegal under the present law of this country. What I will discuss is whether publishing such words should be illegal in a liberal democracy. And I will try to discuss this as moderately and as cautiously as I can.

I say that it should not be illegal to publish such words. In saying this, I am not calling for some libertarian utopia. I am simply asking for a return to the laws that, for many centuries, had policed speech in the England of my birth—in the England, indeed, of my early manhood. I was born into a country where a man could say pretty nearly anything he liked about public issues. He was constrained by the law of obscenity if he wanted to talk about sex, and by the law of official secrecy if he wanted to discuss the confidential workings of government. He might also have been constrained by the law of blasphemy if he wanted to talk about the Christian Faith. Of course, there were also the contempt laws that I have already mentioned. With the exception of the contempt laws, which make sense in any case where a jury might be involved, I will not defend these laws. They constrained speech more than I would have approved had I been old enough to make an informed comment. But, these laws aside, speech was free on public issues.

A man could freely denounce the policing of the Troubles in Ulster. He could praise the Irish Republican Army as "freedom fighters," and rejoice whenever a soldier or policeman was murdered. He could say, for example, that Lord Mountbatten, who was murdered by Irish terrorists in 1980, was "a legitimate target," and hope that some other member of the Royal Family—other than the Queen—might be next. Or, if the inclination took him, he could say that black people were sub-human, and that the Jews were "blood-sucking parasites." He could call a man a "nigger," or—assuming he could prove it—that a man was a "queer" and that he would burn in hell.

On private issues, there were the defamation laws, and the law of confidence. Where threats of violence were concerned, there were the assault laws. For example, if a man said "I know where you live," or "I know where your children go to school," or "You'd better watch yourself as you walk home late in the evening," he might be charged with assault. Words like these, after all, could be taken as threats by any man of reasonable firmness of mind.

Moving back to the public sphere, a man might be charged with a breach of the peace if he turned up outside a synagogue and told a crowd that gentile children inside were being made into Passover cakes.

Now, some of these laws were, as said, absurdly harsh. Others made good sense. But there was never any question that jokes in poor taste might be illegal. I remember reading an article once in *The Spectator* where Auberon Waugh called for a television producer to be put up against a wall and shot. Some people laughed. Others scowled. There was never any question that the police might be involved.

England is now a country where virtually any words uttered in public can be treated as a criminal offence. Without thinking very hard, I can remember how Nick Griffin of the British National Party stood trial for having called Islam "a wicked vicious faith."[61] I can remember how a drunken student was arrested and fined for telling a policeman that his horse looked "gay."[62] I can remember how a man was arrested and charged and fined for standing beside the Cenotaph and reading out the names of the British war dead in Iraq.[63] I remember a case from this year where a pacifist unfurled a banner outside an army cadet training base. "Stop training murderers," it said.[64] His home was promptly raided by police with dogs, while a helicopter hovered overhead. He was arrested and cautioned.

If I started mentioning the cases where Christian street preachers have been arrested for quoting the Bible, or where Moslems have set the police on people for alleged words or displays, or if I even alluded to the Public

---

[61] *www.dailymail.co.uk/news/article-414343/BNP-leader-said-Islam-wicked.html*

[62] *mangans.blogspot.com/2005/06/man-arrested-for-calling-police-horse.html*

[63] *www.telegraph.co.uk/news/uknews/1515599/Protester-fined-for-naming-Gulf-war-dead-at-Cenotaph.html*

[64] *www.thisislondon.co.uk/standard/article-23796444-police-use-dogs-and-helicopter-to-swoop-on-pacifist-student.do*

Order Act or the various racial and sexual hate speech laws, this article would swell immensely. It is enough to say that anything said in public is now illegal if someone complains to the police, or if the police themselves take against it. And, when something is not illegal, we are all getting used to the idea—second nature in most other countries—that we should "watch ourselves." Even I find that, if I discuss politics in a coffee bar, I sometimes drop my voice. A few weeks ago, I found myself looking round to see who might be within earshot. So much for living in a free country.

I am willing to believe that Mrs Alibhai-Brown was put in fear of her life by this tweet. But Mrs Alibhai-Brown may not be a woman of reasonable firmness of mind. Some years ago, she appeared to agree with me in a BBC discussion programme that it was only fear of the law that kept white people from rising up and murdering non-whites[65]. Anyone inclined to doubt this claim should listen to the recording.[66] But no reasonable man can regard the twitter as other than a joke.

I could go po-faced here, and say that it was a joke in questionable taste, or that it was "unacceptable." But a joke is a joke. Often, a joke's humour comes entirely from its being offensive. In a liberal democracy—which this country plainly no longer is—jokes are not a matter for the police. In a country where everyone in public life has not gone barking mad, jokes are heard and laughed at or ignored. It is only in countries that have turned, or are turning, totalitarian that jokes are taken seriously enough for criminal penalties to be threatened.

I could note that this latest outrage has taken place in a country with a Conservative Government. But there is no point. Labour may be out of power, but the Cameron Government is conservative in name only. We should know by now that all the talk during the general election about rolling back the Labour police state was nothing but talk, and that there is no intention to change anything.

I could put it on the record that, as a libertarian, I believe in freedom of speech, and that every law made since 1965 to censor speech should be repealed at once—the Race Relations Acts, the relevant sections of the Public Order Act, and all the dozens of oppressive laws made by the ex-Communists of the Blair and Brown Governments. I might also mention

---

[65] *www.libertarian.co.uk/news/nr015.htm*

[66] *www.libertarian.co.uk/multimedia/2004-02-16-sig-race-1b.mp3*

all the anti-discrimination laws and the obscenity laws. But this is for the record, and I have now put it on the record, and feel there is nothing more to be done for the moment.

No, I think the real villains here are the police. Every so often, *The Daily Mail* publishes a whining article or letter about how the police are kept from doing a proper job by health and safety laws and by "political correctness." The implication here is that the police are thoroughly decent people who simply want to get back to protecting life and property in ways that nearly everyone regards as legitimate. I find this a ludicrous opinion. So far as I can tell, the police are the willing militia of an evil ruling class. Many of them are sadistic thugs more to be feared than the criminals they are supposedly hired to catch. Many are corrupt. Most of them have bought wholesale into the new order of things, and use their massively expanded powers with open and increasingly safe delight.

The police behave as they do partly because of the "tough new laws" Home Secretaries have been drooling over for the past quarter century. But it is also because police officers are bad people. Even if police powers could be rolled back to where they were in about 1960, these traditional powers would still be used oppressively. Power is restrained in part by law. Beyond that, it is restrained by common sense and common decency. These are qualities now absent from the police in England, and no changes in law or exhortations from the top can bring them back. Anyone who wants all the policing our taxes buy needs his head examined.

There is no doubt that all those High Tory critics of Robert Peel were right about the dangers of setting up a state police force. It took over a hundred and fifty years to show how right they were. But, when someone is arrested for making jokes about Yasmin Alibhai-Brown, we can see that the line has been crossed that separates a state with police from a police state.

REFLECTIONS ON THE
CASE OF SUBHAAN YOUNIS (2005)[67]

While having coffee with Dr Tame yesterday [28th September 2005], I did a brief telephone interview with BBC Radio Oxford. The issue I was called on to discuss was whether it was right for a certain Subhaan Younis to be sent to prison for sixty days for having shown someone a video clip on his mobile telephone of a beheading in Iraq.

My answer to the question was no. I agreed that to seek out and take pleasure in such images showed a singular depravity of mind. I also agreed that to show such images to someone who had not agreed in advance to look at them was at least in bad taste. But I disagreed with the man's being sent to prison. By all means, I said, let him be named. Let others know the depravity of his mind, and let him be shunned by the respectable on account of that. But no one should be punished for merely looking at or even publishing things that others might find offensive.

Of course, there is the matter of procurement. If this man had commissioned the beheading so that he might look at pictures of it, it would be right to prosecute him as an accessory to murder. However, so long as no such connection could be shown, he should not be sent to prison.

Then there is the matter of showing the images to someone who had not consented to look at them. According to the newspaper reports, the person to whom they were shown was shocked and upset. Here, though, while there might be some question of an action for the tort of nervous shock, I fail to see anything that ought to be regarded as a criminal matter. Mr Younis should not be in prison. He should be released now he is there.

And that was the whole of my radio discussion. I spoke clearly and firmly, and no one asked me any hard questions. In any event, the whole item took up only about five minutes, and there was no room to develop a full argument or to answer full objections. All I managed in the time was to outline the distinction, on which libertarians mostly insist,

---

[67] First published on *www.seangabb.co.uk* on the 29th September 2005.

Reflections on the Case of Subhaan Younis

between doing and looking. But there is more to be said—as I realised afterwards in a long dissection of the issues with Dr Tame. Indeed, the Younis case is of little importance compared with the larger issues into which its discussion leads.

Let us begin with the question of whether Mr Younis had committed any act that should be regarded as criminal. There is an exception as regards acts against the whole community. But where common crimes are concerned, it is fair to insist that when no individual victim can be identified, there can be no crime. I have no idea what motivated Mr Younis to show that image. He might have been trying to illustrate the horrors of Moslem terrorism. Or he might have believed in the accurate presentation of reality—as opposed to the sanitised, or censored, imagery provided on British television. But his name is Asiatic, and he could be one of those citizens of convenience—that is, someone who values his British passport purely for the material comforts to which it entitles him, who does not share our national ways, and who knows enough about us only to hate us. If so—and I say at once I have no evidence to believe it really is—he would fall into that large class of persons whose presence among us is becoming a problem that needs at least to be honestly discussed.

However, this being raised, let us put it aside and concentrate on whether he can be regarded as a common criminal. Here, we need to identify a victim. It was not Mr Younis himself. His possible moral corruption is not so much effect of the video clip as cause of the faults that led him to seek it out in the first place. So how about the woman to whom he showed the image? Can she be called the victim of an assault?

I do not think so. Mr Younis showed her something that she found upsetting. But let us be reasonable. What he showed her was most likely a jerky, pixellated video clip, and it must have been displayed on a screen of no more than one inch by one and a half. Any person of reasonably firm mind should have been more upset by a good newspaper report. Even applying the civil burden of proof, in making out the tort of nervous shock, I do not think it reasonable for him to have anticipated so extreme a reaction. Unless the accounts I have read of the incident have left out something important, I fail to see how showing that video clip could have been taken as an assault—or even the breach of the peace for which he was punished.

Freedom of Speech in England

The publisher and viewer of the clip being excluded as victims, let us turn instead to the unfortunate subject of the clip. Can we say that Mr Younis had in any sense procured his beheading? As said, there is no doubt that the direct procurement of images that show illegal acts should in itself be a crime. If I have a man killed for the sake of having his death filmed, I ought rightly to be charged as an accessory to murder. But how about what may be called indirect procurement—that is to say, how about acts that fall short of commissioning a criminal act, but which still contribute by a possible chain of inference to the committing of similar acts in the future?

I am at least dubious of this kind of reasoning, but am not required here to enter into close discussion. There is nothing in the newspaper reports to show that Mr Younis had paid to obtain his video clip. Nor is there any reasonable chance that the Iraqi resistance group had beheaded someone with a view to selling the video footage. Nevertheless, while there is no reason to assume any financial incentive, the footage was released in order to attract approval and support outside the resistance group.

Does Mr Younis support the Iraqi resistance? Did he approve of the beheading? The newspaper reports I have seen give no answer to these questions, and I have no evidence for thinking greater ill of him than I do for simply possessing and showing the video clip. But let us for the sake of argument suppose that he does support the Iraqi resistance, and that his support was quickened by sight of the beheading. Does this change matters? Could it be argued that the intention of the beheaders to gain approval and his granting of public approval did create a sufficient *nexus* to justify an accusation of indirect procurement?

I do not think so. It may be wrong to support the various groups resisting the American and British occupation of Iraq, and to glorify their acts. But this must be regarded as fair comment on events of public importance. To magnify any such comment with video clips of an atrocity is irrelevant. I know that the British Government is trying to create a new offence that will cover expressions of support for irregular political violence. But this is political censorship. It is the modern equivalent of the seditious libel laws that were used in the 1790s to stifle the support of some English radicals for the French Revolution. If applied consistently, the proposed law—indeed, the breach of the peace law used to punish Mr Younis—could be used to punish my own view that the Iraqi resistance groups stand in a tradition that leads through the *Guerillas* of the Peninsula War and the French Resistance of living memory. To answer yes to the above question is to sanction as close a censorship of the media as we have known in this country since the expiry of the Licensing Act.

But while I think I have answered the specific question of whether Mr Younis should have been sent to prison for showing that video clip, I have done so in a way that avoids what Dr Tame and I take as the wider and much more interesting question—of whether any possession or publication should in themselves be treated as crimes. What happened yesterday to Mr Younis was an act of disguised censorship, and I can join with the media class in deploring this. But I am drawn to discuss it by the general principle that some are using to justify his punishment. Should possession or publication be treated as crimes in themselves?

I do not think so. As I said yesterday about Mr Younis, where no connection can be shown to its original creation, there should be no crime in publication. Or, where no aggression can be identified, no crime can be imputed. The argument that buying what is already in being encourages the creation of more is invalid, so far as it muddles the necessary distinction between identifiable and prospective victims.

There is also the argument of procedural honesty—that to make a crime of possession is to give the police even greater scope for corrupt and oppressive behaviour than they otherwise enjoy. To prove an offence of procurement or publication usually requires objective evidence that is difficult to fabricate. To prove an offence of possession requires the unsupported word of a police officer or some agent of provocation. I do not think, at this late stage in our national decline, I need to bother with arguing that the police are corrupt and oppressive. It is notorious that the police in this country have a long history of "stitching up" individuals by planting whatever items may currently be demonised. Anyone who believes they are uniformed civilians, paid to do the job that we might, if so inclined, do for ourselves of protecting life and property, has never read a newspaper.

Furthermore I think it highly dangerous to go any further than we so far have in the granting of extraterritorial jurisdiction. We have gone too far already. Unless we are to consent to the growth of an unaccountable and increasingly tyrannical body of international criminal law, we should insist on principle that acts committed elsewhere in the world ought not to be the business of our own criminal courts. For the same reason we should insist that those accused of criminal acts in this country should

Freedom of Speech in England

not be extradited to face trial elsewhere in the world—and that therefore our Government should refuse to implement the European Arrest Warrant, and should denounce the treaty signed a few years back with the United States of America.

I suspect most of my readers will agree with these two last points. But there are problems with the refusal to countenance any extra-territorial jurisdiction. Does this mean that, if a man living in this country should directly procure the filming of a terrorist act in France, he should not be subject to prosecution in this country? Does it mean that Egyptian nationals living in this country should be able with impunity to procure the assassination of the Egyptian President in their own country?

With regard to the second question, I can argue that, as a matter of policy, we should not allow foreigners into this country who are likely to complicate our foreign relations. And any who are found plotting here should be expelled at once—regardless of what punishment they can expect in their own countries. But answering the first question is difficult. Before the law was changed in 1858, in response to the Orsini bomb plot, there was no crime of conspiring to break the laws of another country. Nor, until the Fugitive Offenders Act of later in the century, was there any means of sending suspects from this country to face trial in another country.

I sympathise with the old concept of an absolutely separate territorial jurisdiction. On the other hand, the concept was applied in a world where, having regard to the state of communications, France was more distant from England than China is today. Paris is now within a three hour railway journey from Waterloo Station, and the price of telephone calls to anywhere in the world is heading toward zero. Perhaps the concept is no longer applicable in its strict sense. Perhaps, then, there is a case for laws to punish the direct procurement of crimes in another country. This would cover publishers who commission terrorist pornography from anywhere in the world. It would also cover people—such as Mr Younis is almost certainly not—whose approval of terrorist acts abroad amounts to commissioning. As said, such laws might not cover Mr Younis. But they would cover those hyphenated Americans who have spent the past forty years contributing financially to the Fenian insurrection in Ulster.

But this takes me further from the case of Mr Younis than I intended to go. I will conclude by repeating that he should not have been sent to prison on the basis of the facts reported in the newspapers. Nor should he have been sent there on the basis of any argument I have seen made or can imagine being made. I do not know Mr Younis. I have no sympathy for him. But this is irrelevant to the question of his punishment. What is relevant is to recall the words of John Lilburne as he was led out to punishment: "What they do to me today, they may do to any man tomorrow."

Mr Younis should be released.

How not to Stop the London Bombings: In Defence of Liberal Democracy (1999)[68]

Should organisations that preach racial hatred be banned and their members put in prison? "Yes" says a body called the National Assembly Against Racism. "Yes" say various politicians and journalists. I have just returned home from arguing "no" on the Edwina Currie show on BBC Radio Five; and since I did rather well in defence of liberal democracy, I have decided to repeat myself in print.

Before doing so, however, I must bear in mind that many of my readers do not live in England, and some will be living in the more or less distant future. For their sake, I will explain the background to this turn in the debate over political censorship.

April 1999 was a bad month for Londoners. We had the most concentrated burst of armed violence since the Irish terror campaign of the mid-1970s. On Saturday the 17th, a nail bomb was let off in Brixton—a largely black area in South West London—injuring several people. On Saturday the 24th, another nail bomb was let off in a largely Asian part of East London, again injuring several people. On Monday the 26th, a television presenter was shot dead on her doorstep in West London.[69] Then on Friday the 30th another nail bomb was let off in a gay pub in the West End of London, killing three people and causing dozens of horrible injuries.

Nothing is known yet about the shooting, but the bombings appear to be the work of a national socialist organisation calling itself the White Wolves. It has published a few warnings to the usual objects of hatred, telling them to leave the country before the end of the year. At first, I suspected this was the work of the security services, trying to justify their existence now that the Cold War is over and that the Government has

---

[68] First published on *www.seangabb.co*.uk on the 2nd May 1999.

[69] This was Jill Dando. When nobody came forward and told them whom to arrest, the police fitted up a mental defective called Barry George. He served several years for the murder, before being let out with inadequate compensation. (Note supplied, August 2013)

surrendered to the IRA. But the sight of Gerry Gable—"this country's most eminent anti-fascist"—looking honestly taken by surprise has persuaded me that the White Wolves really do exist.

The reaction following from this seems plain enough to me. I feel sorry for the victims. I hope the Police will soon catch the perpetrators. I hope the courts will punish them to the full degree allowed by law. In the meantime, I plan to avoid crowded places so far as is convenient. And that is all.

The "anti-racists," though, do not agree. Their agenda has nothing to do with freedom and equality, but instead is one of censorship and political tyranny; and they have taken the bombings as an excuse to advance that agenda. One day, I will sit down and write at length about their motivations.[70] For now, I will just say that "anti-racism" is a doctrine shared by self-hating whites, black and brown racists, and the stupid and the nasty and the dishonestly ambitious of all colours.

It was to defend liberal democracy against these people that I sat down last night in Broadcasting House and argued for two hours. The case I put can be summarised as follows:

Freedom of speech is the most precious freedom that can ever be possessed. The right freely to speak, to write, to publish, and to learn what others have to say, is central to our existence as rational beings. It is also the means by which other freedoms are given meaning and are preserved from attack. Take that away, or seriously abridge it, and all else can and will also be taken. For this reason, no opinion is ever to be suppressed. That opinion may be absurd. It may be grossly offensive. It may recommend the most dangerous or alarming things. But this is of no importance. Freedom of speech is well worth the disadvantages that may sometimes attend its use.

I accept the occasional need for limiting the means of expressing certain opinions. This makes me a moderate within the libertarian movement: I have friends whose defence of free speech is much more absolutist, and perhaps they are right and I am wrong. But at the moment, it does strike me as reasonable to allow in principle for some restrictions regarding time and place and manner of expression.

---

[70] I did in 2007: *Cultural Revolution, Culture War: How Conservatives Have Lost England and How to Get it Back*, Hampden Press, London.

Freedom of Speech in England

Take, for example, someone who turns up outside a synagogue one Saturday morning and starts abusing the congregation. That is an act likely to cause a breach of the peace. As such, it may rightly be controlled by law. Or take someone who incites offences against life or property at a time when he knows that his listeners are already out of their right minds. He is then using those people as an instrument of his will, rather as if he were pulling the strings of a puppet. Here also are grounds for control—for holding the inciter partly responsible for what he has incited.

Again, widening the debate to include pornography or blasphemy, or whatever else may be found offensive, it is often proper to insist that certain publications should be made available only in private for those who have specifically gone looking for them, and that the majority should not be needlessly reminded of their existence and so provoked into calls for censorship.

But the "anti-racists" are not interested in limiting means of expression. They want to try suppressing whole opinions. They would like a blanket censorship, treating scientific journals and private conversations in exactly the same way as public meetings. Anyone who puts arguments about freedom of speech or due process of law is told to "get a life in the real world." Their excuse is that any manner of expressing what they do not like contributes in some way to a "climate of opinion" in which bombings and other acts of violence become accepted as legitimate. Their argument is absurd for two reasons:

First, the London bombings are less an effect of liberal tolerance than of previous efforts at censorship. For at least the past 25 years, national socialists and racists have been excluded from political debate in this country. When they are allowed into the broadcast media, they are recorded in advance, and what they say is carefully edited to make them appear in the worst possible light. The planning laws are used to try and shut down their headquarters buildings. They cannot use property owned or controlled by local authorities to hold public meetings. What meetings they do hold are broken up by screaming mobs. The Government is preparing an election law for the London Assembly specifically to stop them from winning any seats. They cannot get jobs in the public sector. They cannot work in universities. If they are found studying at a university, they are lucky if they graduate in one piece and with an indifferent degree. They have fair claim to being called this country's

How Not to Stop the London Bombings

most persecuted minority. Little wonder some of them have turned to violence, the last resort of the excluded.

Anyone who is really interested in discouraging the national socialists from violence—rather then just in suppressing them—should be arguing for their inclusion in normal political debate. I would like to see a spokesman from the British National Party given the same chance that even I have to appear for two hours at a time on live national radio. No one can credibly argue that this would increase their level of support. It might do the opposite. The plain fact is that when these people have been able to put their case without censorship, they have never had any political success in this country. No one has ever been elected to Parliament as a national socialist. They are a political minority even more despised than the Communists used to be. The disinfecting light of publicity would deter the violent extremists among them, and would still further reduce their public support.

Second, I have always found it odd that this climate of opinion talk has only ever been seriously used to justify suppression of the national socialists. International socialism has been far more bloody by every measure. The publication of *The Communist Manifesto* encouraged the murder during this century of more than a hundred million people. Even though the main Communist wave has broken and receded, there are Marxist groups in this country still plotting violent revolution and inciting violence on the streets. Yet *The Communist Manifesto* remains openly on sale, with commentaries by eminent scholars, and is taught to schoolchildren in political science courses. I have never heard calls in this country for the works of Karl Marx to be banned, or for the movements they have inspired to be suppressed. Yet every argument used for censoring the national socialists applies with at least equal force to them.

Much the same can be said about Christianity, Islam, Judaism, Irish nationalism, environmentalism, and the animal rights movement. These have all been associated in recent years in this country with acts of political violence. I would not restrain any of these various movements— but then I believe in punishing people for actual crimes against life and property, not because they might somehow have encouraged such crimes, or because people who claim to support the same cause have committed them. It is worth asking why those who make such a fuss about one very small group have so little regard for consistency. If we are to treat the

Freedom of Speech in England

members of one movement as collectively guilty for the acts of its lunatic fringe, why not so treat the others as well?

These are my arguments, and I put them last night with numerous repetition and variation. I hope they had some effect. I know that I gave great offence to the person I was arguing against. This was one Maximilian Alphonso Hales—approximate spelling—Chairman of the Birmingham and Sandwell Racial Attacks Monitoring Unit. The man came across as embarrassingly stupid. His argument seemed to be that every black or brown person in this country lives under permanent threat of "racial terrorism"—which includes graffiti and rude words as well as the more usual hardships of rape, arson and murder—and that this is all somehow a continuation of "colonialism" when the white man went into Africa "with the *Bible* in one hand and a gun in the other." I tried drawing his attention to the fact that his adopted country was the first in history to abolish slavery and nearly went to war several times in the last century in its efforts to put down the international slave trade. But at the first hint of criticism, Mr Hales exploded with accusations that I was "patronising" him. He was so bad that he was unable to make any relevant summing up at the end of the programme, and Mrs Currie came unexpectedly back to me for a second summing up of my own. I once did a radio discussion with a black feminist who tied me in intellectual knots that might have been exciting had they been physical. But Mr Hales was a sore disappointment. I imagine that somehow or other my taxes pay his salary. If so, I want my money back.

Now, I should turn to the question asked about everyone who opposes the malign doctrine of "anti-racism"—what are my views on race? My answer is that I condemn any judgment passed on individuals solely because of ethnic origin. Individuals ought to be judged on who they are, not what colour they are. I will not say that some of my best friends are black—as Mrs Currie rather slimily tried to press me into claiming—but some of my ordinary friends are black; and I should be surprised if any of my black or brown students thought me at all biased for or against them on account of their colour.

I further believe that the majority of black and brown people in this country do not consider themselves victims of racial terrorism, and do not look to Mr Hales or anyone else in the race relations industry for protection. The majority are honest, law-abiding fellow-citizens. I have found an encouraging number of them share my fears about the absorption of this country into a European superstate. Indeed, if I were leader of the Conservative Party, I would be making every effort to pick up votes among the ethnic minorities—not, as Mr Hague is doing, by parroting the lies of the race relations industry, but by appealing to the traditional conservative values of self-help, respectability and patriotism. Do this, and the Tories might start winning parliamentary elections in places like Brixton and Tottenham.

But, as said, I have done my little bit this weekend for liberal democracy.

.

The Latest Shootings in America: An English View (2011)[71]

I try to avoid commenting on American affairs. It is usually bad manners to get involved in the politics of a foreign country. It is always unwise for someone to get involved in the politics of country where he does not live. I see this all the time in foreign comments on England—they are never enlightening, but range between repetitions of platitude and the utterly perverse. This being said, the shooting last week by Jared Loughner of Gabrielle Giffords, a politician there, and of several other people, is an exception. The matter of who kills whom in America, and for what reason, is no proper concern of mine. But the shootings have, on both sides of the Atlantic, begun a debate over the possible effects of speech on action. So far as this debate touches on England, and might be used to justify the removal of what freedom we still possess, I do not think it inappropriate to comment on the shootings.

Now, when speaking about the removal of our freedoms, a good place to begin is an article in yesterday's *Independent*. Mary Ann Sieghart appears to blame the shootings on freedom of speech. She certainly disapproves of those journalists in America who fail to agree with their ruling class on every main issue. She says, for example:

> These viewers [of Fox News] were shockingly misinformed. They were twice as likely to believe that most scientists don't believe in climate change and that it wasn't clear whether Obama was born in America. The more often they viewed Fox News, the more likely they were to believe these untruths. And the effect wasn't just a matter of partisan bias. Even Democrats who watched the station were more likely to be misinformed.[72]

This is, I must confess, the first good thing I have heard in recent years of any media outlet owned by Rupert Murdoch. For Mrs Sieghart, though, it stands to reason that anything like the spreading of probable

---

[71] First published on *www.seangabb.co.*uk on the 11th January 2011.

[72] Mary Ann Sieghart, "There are Lessons for Us from Arizona," *The Independent*, London, 10th January 2011.

truth on these and other issues must lead inevitably to the shooting of politicians. Such is her opinion, and such seems to be the consensus among other ruling class propagandists here and in America.

I do expect this consensus to fracture in the next few days. In America, media attention may be shifted to the supposed ease with which common people can buy guns. Over here, this would be the waste of a good shooting. Our victim disarmament laws are already about the strictest in the world. The only way left to reduce the number of guns in circulation would be to start disarming criminals and the police. But, though our own censorship laws are also stricter than the American, they are still far from complete. Every so often, there are reports in the newspapers that someone has been arrested for uttering words that might, before about 1980, barely have raised an eyebrow; and libertarians of all shades—real libertarians, that is, not the sort who get jobs with *The Guardian* or the BBC—then strike up a chorus of horror about the abolition of free speech. We are, of course, right in one sense. On the other hand, the censorship laws are still applied very feebly, and they do not apply to dissent within the educated classes. So long as we know what phrasing to avoid, we can still complain as we please about the joint loss of our country and of our liberties. Stopping this is much more important to our ruling class than finding an excuse to take away a few more shotguns and hunting rifles. It therefore makes sense for the debate in England over these shootings to remain fixed on the alleged connection between what is called hate speech and violent crime.

Already, the newspapers here are repeating claims about the influence on Jared Loughner of the white nationalist journal *American Renaissance*.[73] According to a headline in the last *Mail on Sunday*, "Tucson shooting suspect [is] linked to fanatical pro-white magazine with anti-Semitic and anti-government views."[74] The story is repeated across much of the British media. It is only a matter of time before someone points out that Nick Griffin, leader of the British National Party, was invited to speak last year at an *American Renaissance* conference—and would have spoken, had this not been cancelled after threats of violence from "anti-fascist" protestors. We shall then have a "clear and obvious" connection between Mr Griffin and Jared Loughner. It may be

---

[73] *http://www.amren.com/*

[74] *The Mail on Sunday*, London, 9th January 2011.

remembered how, in 1999, someone called David Copeland let off several bombs in London. He had briefly been a member of the BNP. Though he had left the moment he discovered that no one shared his interest in killing people, calls still went up for the party to be banned. The calls were manifestly unfair. The BNP could be held no more responsible for David Copeland's crimes than the Social Democratic Party could for the crimes of the serial sex killer Dennis Nilsen. But that was then. The BNP is now the third or fourth opposition party in this country. I have no doubt the calls will go up again. I do not think they will fade away so quickly.

But let us look at this "fanatical" and "anti-semitic" and "anti-government" and pro-white" journal. Anyone who looks on the *American Renaissance* website will see that it is a white nationalist journal. Its overall message is to claim that whites should think of themselves as members of a distinct group, with certain interests and certain aptitudes, and that they should defend their possession of those territories where they now form the majority—and that they should be at least sceptical when members of other groups, or their white allies, call for endless apology and abasement and surrender.

These claims may be true. They may be false. They may equally be irrelevant in a world where a set of cultural values and ways of thinking about the world may have first been developed by whites, but are now the common heritage of all mankind, and where future conflicts will arise not between whites and non-whites, but between believers and disbelievers in the power and autonomy of reason. Civilisation, as it has so far existed, may be overwhelmingly a creation of the white races. But that may not be so in the future. Political correctness and forced multi-culturalism should be denounced as ruling class legitimation strategies. But a libertarian world, based on respect for life, liberty and property, will have its own natural diversity.

But true or false or irrelevant, I can see nothing in *American Renaissance* that could be remotely described as an incitement to violence. The tone of the journal is uniformly courteous and scholarly. I have never once seen the slightest intemperance of language, except where it has been necessary to quote the words of others. It is not fanatical. It is certainly not anti-Semitic. Some of its writers are Jews. So are many of its readers. If some borderline raving lunatic can read a copy of *American Renaissance*, and find in it advice that he should go out and shoot someone, that is properly a matter for the lawyers and doctors to

The Latest Shootings in America: An English View

consider, not an excuse for censorship of the journal or the persecution of its readers.

The standard response to this sort of factual challenge is to collapse all distinctions between incitement and inspiration, and to carry into the second the moral blame attached to the first. We saw this in 1999, when no one could find evidence that the BNP had recommended any acts of violence. The talk then was all of the "climate of hate" variety. The BNP was said to have created an environment within which acts of violence were more likely to be perceived as legitimate. The same argument is used by the anti-pornography lobby. No one can prove that showing pictures of naked women is direct incitement to rape. And so the claim is that these pictures somehow "dehumanise" all women and make it more likely that they will be raped.

Whoever uses it, this argument is based on a trick. Incitements to violence imply blame. Inspiration at worst implies causality. Anyone who uses the argument must be a villain or a fool. Most who use it, I am sure, are villains. They are villains because they never apply it consistently. For example, I have never read the collected writings of Marx and Engels. What I have read, though, does not contain any direct incitement to mass-enslavement and mass-murder. However, they are a strong mix of denunciation and utopian fantasy that have obviously inspired the creation of terrorist governments. Again, the reported words of Christ suggest a more than womanly dislike of violence. But his promise of eternal life for all who will heed his call to repentance has been inspiring various kinds of inquisition for the past two thousand years. Should we therefore use the "climate of hate argument" to ban *Das Capital* or shut down the Roman Catholic Church? I do not think any of the ruling class propagandists who will cry up the alleged link between Jared Loughner and Nick Griffin *via* Jared Taylor will show much interest in consistency. They want to make the BNP an illegal organisation, and any argument—no matter how defective—will do, so long as they can get enough people to go along with it.

But let us leave the matter of inspiration and go back to arguments about incitement. Let us suppose—and this is not, I believe, the case—that *American Renaissance* and Nick Griffin and the BNP were to advocate the use of violence. Should this be made grounds for any kind of legal action against them? Again, I will say that this case is hypothetical: it has neither evidence nor other credibility. But let it be supposed for the sake of argument. I think the answer must be no. Someone who commissions violent acts against a named individual is an accessory to the crime, and there is no need to consider the nature or degree of incitement. It may be a special case when a man is urging on an angry crowd against some nearby object. But someone who makes a speech inside a room, or who writes a book or an article—especially if no names are mentioned or implied, and if no money changes hands—should not be held legally responsible if others take his words, even if in their most natural meaning, and go out and hurt someone. The sole responsibility for acts of violence must lie with those who commit them. This is so because all reasonable considerations make it so. A man who reads or hears an argument for violence will generally have enough time before carrying words into action to think about what he is doing, and to take responsibility. Deny this, and you have to say that Bill Gates forced me to buy Windows 7 because, three weeks after he offered me a copy for £30, I pulled out a credit card and paid the money—or that Margaret Thatcher forced David Laws to give the taxpayers' money to his male lover, because she first allowed House of Commons expenses to become a shadow increase of salary for Members of Parliament.

Moreover, to make a crime of incitement is to deny the possibility of democratic government. If men cannot be trusted to think for themselves, it is both dangerous and a waste of time to trust them with the vote. Of course, this may be a good argument against the sort of democracy we now have. But anyone who really does believe in our current political system should be cautious about accepting any argument that spreads responsibility for criminal acts beyond those who commit them.

I am not saying it is other than disreputable for someone to preach violence against those he dislikes. There is a case for shunning people like Abu Hamza. I just do not see how it can be consistent with any idea of liberal democracy to hold one man guilty of crimes committed by another. But—I repeat—I am not accusing any of the persons mentioned of incitement. I only deny that incitement is the excuse for censorship it is taken to be.

As I have said, what happens in America is not my concern. It is not my country. I have no regard for the United States as a country or as an idea. Equally, as said, when American facts seem likely to be made into argument for the further theft of English liberties, I do see reason for commenting on those facts. All that remains is to see whether the debate in England goes in the direction that I strongly suspect it will.

THOUGHTS ON EMMA WEST:
HOW TO ARGUE WITH
THE RULING CLASS (2011)[75]

One of the ways in which a ruling class keeps control is its insistence on rules of debate that place opposition at a regular disadvantage. I cannot think of any time or place where opposition voices have been listened to on fully equal terms. In modern England, however, the ruling class and its various clients and useful idiots are particularly rigid in their shepherding of debate. This is so not only because England is an increasingly totalitarian place, but also because the main legitimation ideologies are all obviously false and cannot be exposed to open criticism. Therefore, while speech mostly remains free in the legal sense, it will only be listened to when expressed in terms that privilege the ruling class.

Some of the rules of debate in England are linguistic. For example, if you refer to someone as a homosexual, you will be told that he is gay. Or you will be told that the Indian cities of Bombay and Calcutta must be called "Mumbai" and "Kolkata;" or that the native population of England must be called the "white majority;" or an immigrant a "migrant," or a failed suicide a "self-harmer," or a mongol a "Downs syndrome sufferer." If you persist in using the now disapproved words, you may be dismissed as ignorant: you may be denounced as some kind of bigot. Sometimes, the words keep changing, or different words must be used depending on the audience—therefore, "Ethiopian" became "person of colour," and then "negro," and then "Negro," and then "coloured," and then "black," and then "Afro-Caribbean," and may still be any of these except possibly "coloured." In many cases, names are changed merely when something pejorative is replaced by something neutral—obviously

---

[75] First published on *www.seangabb.co.uk* on the 5th December 2011. Once she insisted that she would plead not guilty to the offences with which she was charged, Miss West's trial was repeatedly delayed. After eighteen months, however, she did plead guilty. Accepting that she had been drunk and drugged and generally not in her right mind, the Judge bound her over for twelve months to keep the peace. So justice is done in a soft totalitarian police state.

so in the instance just given. More often, though, the changes are made to humble those outside the naming *élite*. Whoever must follow the other side's naming conventions loses any claim to equality of status, and will at least tend to lose any debate. This is so when the shift of name is mostly verbal—for example coloured to black. But it is specially so when the shift involves an acceptance of new facts. See again the shift from "native English" to "white majority." The former implies that a particular territory is historically the possession of a self-defined group, and suggests that this group has a right to continue in possession. The latter simply implies that one group among many has what may be a passing numerical weight. Equally, "migration" is so much softer and less threatening than "immigration." Quibbling over words may sound petty. But to control the words usable in debate really is to have a very great if subtle advantage in debate.

A similar advantage is had by taking real or pretended offence, and calling on an opponent to apologise. When those crying out in horror have numbers or the power of government on their side, they can avoid the danger of arguing with an opponent by smashing his reputation. People are led to believe that he is a bad person. Often the person himself can be brought to agree. We saw how this can work last week. Speaking on a BBC programme that lies on the border between news and light entertainment, Jeremy Clarkson said that strikers in the public sector should be shot. No one but a fool could believe he intended this as other than a joke. But it raised a storm of synthetic outrage. The BBC gave in at once and apologised for any offence caused. Mr Clarkson may or may not have apologised, but certainly did not stand his ground. His enemies are now circulating rumours that his mind is unbalanced, and the credibility of a prominent non-conformist may have been destroyed.

Or there are demands for "historic apologies." The Celtic peoples are rather good at this. So are the Indians. Peter Tatchell made an effort last month to get the Prime Minister to apologise for the criminalisation of homosexual acts throughout the British Empire.[76] He failed. But demanding apologies for alleged ill-treatment in the past is a good way to advance present interests. It smoothes the way to actual financial or legal advantages. Or—as with the Irish—it just wins battles in a long-term vendetta.

---

[76] Peter Tatchell, "Cameron should apologise for anti-gay laws," *The Pink News*, London, 4th November 2011.

Thoughts on Emma West

Or there is the hiding of rights violations behind the grief of victims. Last week, for example, I put out my annual call for the repeal of the laws against drinking and driving. My argument is that the dangers of drinking and driving are much exaggerated—the published statistics are puffed up by including cases where drunken pedestrians or cyclists have got themselves knocked down. The present law is only enforced by stopping drivers at random and breathalysing them. This is a breach of the old common law rule against interference with individuals except with probable cause. Most of the people stopped do not test positive. Most of those who do test positive were not driving erratically. Enforcement also takes the police away from their—admittedly casual—protection of life and property. It would be better, I say, to punish drivers who are caught driving without proper care and attention, or who have hurt others, and to make sure that the punishments are harsh enough to deter.

I may be wrong about this. Perhaps the current law is the only way to keep the roads as safe as they are. Whatever the case, I nearly always find myself going on the wireless to debate with the grieving relatives of people killed by drunken drivers. Many years ago, I gave a blunt response to one of these people—that, while private grief must always be respected, it has no claim to respect when dragged into debates over law or policy of state. This sent everyone else in the studio into a self-righteous frenzy, and got my microphone turned off. My favourite response is to sympathise, and to show that, if I were given my way, the guilty driver would have been locked away for life, or even hanged. Usually, this gives me the advantage of surprise. Even so, I still have to ask for the moral endorsement of someone who is arguing for a police state.

And this brings me to what I really want to discuss—which is the demand for argument by supplication. Last week, Emma West was filmed swearing at a tram filled with black people. She was immediately punished by having her life destroyed. For those who, for whatever reason, have not heard about her, this brief statement of mine gives the main story:

> Emma West is a white working class woman who got into an argument with some black people in a South London Tram. A video of what she said was posted on YouTube. She has now been arrested for her opinions and locked away, and her children have been taken away by the social services.

Freedom of Speech in England

> Of course, if she had been wearing a headscarf and screeching about the "kuffar" who were killing her brothers and sisters in Iraq/Afghanistan, the authorities would have looked the other way.
>
> For a woman to have her children taken away because she expressed opinions disliked by the ruling class means we have come as close as doesn't matter to a totalitarian police state. I note that this has happened under a "Conservative" Government. Where are all those "Tory" MPs who like to preen themselves on how libertarian they are? Don't ask.
>
> My view is that every single politician and official involved in this arrest of a dissident and legalised kidnapping of her children should be punished after the collapse of the present *régime*—not only sacked and deprived of pension rights (because they all will be in the disestablishment of the ruling class), but also made jointly and severally liable for compensating Miss West and her children for whatever they may have suffered.

I have quoted this in full not only because it gives the main facts of the case, but also because it brought a response that I was hoping to provoke someone into making. It came last Friday:

> Sean
>
> While the punishment meted out to this racist idiot is indeed unacceptable what is remarkable is that you should spring to her defence without disassociating yourself clearly from the contemptible views she espouses. More remarkable still is that you propose that every politician and official involved should be punished, deprived of their pension rights and held liable for compensating Miss West
>
> Scratch a "free market anti-statist" and you will invariably find a statist lurking within
>
> For non-market anti-statist socialism
>
> Xxxxx Yyy

Now, the writer of this is not a member of the ruling class. He may or may not be one of its clients. But he certainly comes into the category of useful idiot. Leave aside his assumption that a society can hold together by any other means than voluntary association or compulsion by the State—what interests me is his outrage that I did not join to my defence of Miss West's rights a denunciation of what she said. Increasingly, you are only allowed to defend those persecuted by the ruling class by abasing yourself before the ruling class. Somewhere in what I said, I should have added a variant on the following:

Thoughts on Emma West

> I bow to no one in my utter revulsion of what this evil young guttersnipe said. Being myself a transgendered black lesbian, I have had more than my share of hate-filled bigotry. And I celebrate the immense patience shown by those poor abused people. That no one was driven to violence against West is proof of how strong our diverse and multicultural society has become. All this being said, it is only out of an old-fashioned, and therefore possibly misguided, liberalism that I beg for her not to suffer the full consequences of her totally abhorrent crime against humanity.

Well, I knew that I was expected to come out with this kind of dirt-kissing exercise, and I refused to comply. I refused, because it is inhuman to spit on someone who has already been brought down. I refused because a defence of someone's rights is often compromised by adverse comment on what he has done. The paraphrase on Voltaire—"I disagree with what you say, but would defend to the death your right to say it"—is all very well when arguing with someone on the other side of a dinner table. My own view, when someone is lying on the ground, is to skip the disagreement.

This has always been my practice. In 1991, I wrote the first and one of the best defences of the "Spanner 15"—that is, of the homosexual men who were tried and punished for consensual acts in private: one of them was convicted of "aiding and abetting an assault on himself"![77] Not once in any of the essays I wrote or the speeches I made did I insist that I was not myself a leather-worshipping sado-masochistic homosexual, or that I would not like someone to drive a four inch nail through my penis. I got some very funny looks for this omission. But I refused then to distance myself from powerless and ruined victims of injustice—and I refuse now.

I also refuse because what is demanded of me is an endorsement of a legitimising ideology. Here—and for the sake of clarity alone—I will explain what I think of Miss West's actions. She was vulgar in her speech and uncharitable in her sentiments. But I do not for a moment think that, except for her and people like her, what has been made of my country would be a vibrant love feast without end. While modern commerce and modern technology almost cry out for some mixing of peoples, state-sponsored mass-immigration has been made an excuse to destroy the internal cohesion of my people and to free my rulers from practical accountability. That a quarter of this country's population may now be strangers, who have been encouraged neither to adopt nor even to respect

---

[77] https://www.seangabb.co.uk/free-life-18-may-1993-reflections-on-the-case-of-r-v-brown-by-sean-gabb/

our ways, is a problem to which I can think of no satisfactory answer. But I refuse, when speaking out against their growing intolerance of disagreement, to bow my head to the people who rule this country. They are not good people led astray by bad ideas. They do not occupy any moral high ground. Until such time as they grow more tyrannical than they have yet become, I will avoid arguing with them on their terms. What they have done to us is evil in itself, and, because it is highly unstable, it will almost certainly lead to greater evils. The least bad outcome will be a swift collapse of the *régime* they have created, and their punishment with some regard given to due process. And they deserve no less. They are in a position to know exactly what they are doing. If they have chosen not to make the obvious connections of cause and effect, their ignorance is culpable.

Because, more than is usually the case, it is founded on lies and violence, the present *régime* must eventually collapse. I have no inclination to join some future equivalent of storming the Bastille. Something I can do, though, is to look these people in the face, and refuse to observe their rules of debate. The purpose of these rules is to restrain a debate that would otherwise turn dangerous. No revolution has ever succeeded except after there had been a withdrawal of consent. Let this be withdrawn, and the secret of all power is laid bare—that we are many and they are few. There is little else I will do. But, however small it may be in the overall scheme of things, this much I have done already.

EMMA CHAMBERLAIN AND THE ASTOR THEATRE: HOW DISSIDENTS ARE TREATED IN MODERN ENGLAND (2006)[78]

About a hundred yards from where I live in Deal is the Astor Theatre. A nondescript building in an Edwardian terrace, I walk past it every time I go to the railway station. I used to pay some attention to its forthcoming attractions notices. But these never displayed anything vaguely attractive to me, and I soon stopped paying attention.

The Theatre is now suddenly in the news. The main headline in this week's *Dover Express* reads: "Drama tutor is the 'face' of BNP." Apparently, Emma Chamberlain, who teaches drama classes at the Theatre, is a presenter for the BNPtv news service of the British National Party. This story covers most of the front page and nearly the whole of the inside front. There are photographs of Miss Chamberlain, descriptions of the work she has done for the BNP, and a listing of the sort of things in which the BNP believes—these ranging from deportation of illegal immigrants to resisting the Islamisation of Britain.

The Artistic Director of the Theatre is quoted as not having known that Miss Chamberlain was an active member of the BNP. He expresses his complete confidence in her abilities. He then promises to consult with the Trustees of the Theatre to see if she should be dismissed. Gwyn Prosser, the local Member of Parliament, avoids all pretence of hypocrisy. He insists she should be dismissed for her opinions. He says:

> I look upon the BNP as an evil, right-wing, fascist organisation. Anyone that espouses the beliefs of that party should not have anything to do with young people. If my child were in that class [taught by Miss Chamberlain], I would take them out immediately.

Now, this is an interesting story. It may report events in a part of England that few visit. But can be used to illustrate much that is wrong with modern England as a whole.

---

[78] First published on *www.seangabb.co.uk* on the 14th April 2006.

Freedom of Speech in England

To begin, it is obvious that the story is not really an item of news, and never was intended to be such. It is of no reasonable interest to anyone what may be the opinions of a drama teacher at some obscure theatre that does not appear to take money from the taxpayers. This is not news.

But then, *The Dover Express* is not really a newspaper. Despite its name, and despite its correspondence address, the publication is owned by Trinity Mirror plc. This, according to its website, publishes "over 75 free and paid for titles in London and the south east of England." Its overriding objective is to make money from advertising. Even when there is a cover price on one of its publications, advertising revenue makes up at least half the total revenue—and often very much more than that. The gathering of local news is not a priority for any of the titles owned by Trinity Mirror. It is something to be done as cheaply as possible and with as little friction as possible.

These facts make just about every local newspaper into a client of its local authority. A large fraction of its advertising is from the local authority— jobs, tenders, notices and the like. Local authority advertising does not require much soliciting. Invoices to local authorities are usually paid on time, and are usually paid on good rates per line or word. The same is true of the news. This can be gathered very cheaply by reporters sat in their offices and sifting through the weekly harvest of news releases. Most stories are rewritten releases. And most of these releases come from the various departments of the local authority.

It would be commercial folly for a local newspaper to do other than the bidding of its local authority. Any disobedience brings the threat of no more advertising and no more news releases. Chris Tame once explained to me just how effective this threat can be. When he was working as a press officer for Lambeth Borough Council, he was given the job of stopping the local newspapers from breaking a story that would have embarrassed several Councillors and senior administrators. Someone had videoed a youth from whatever borstals are now called having sex with his mother. The video showed identifiable other parties touching the couple during the sexual act and masturbating. You would think this was hot news. You would think any newspaper would go through every court in the land to defend its reporters and its right to publish their findings. Not so. It took Chris barely an hour to get back every copy of the video. He even got to keep his own copy. All he had to do in each case was threaten the advertising manager.

Emma Chamberlain and the Astor Theatre

This was not an isolated case. Local government has always and in all parts of England been an opportunity for gross corruption; and the local newspapers have generally helped cover things up. More recently, though, local newspapers have been recruited into what the Marxist thinker Louis Althusser called "the ideological state apparatus." They do not simply maintain the fiction that local politicians are men of good character. They also now act as propaganda fronts for the ruling class of which these local politicians are junior members. They carry stories that validate or reinforce the claims of the ruling class. They carry attacks on the enemies of the ruling class. We have a ruling class that wants a complete transformation of the ways in which this country is governed and of the ways in which ordinary people think and associate. Its project is the creation of a politically correct dictatorship. Because this project is fundamentally against human nature, it must be actively propagandised to the point where nothing in any media outlet can be regarded as other than political—nothing, that is, short of the weather reports and football scores. And anyone opposed to the project must be ruthlessly smeared and otherwise destroyed.

That is the real purpose of this story. Dover District Council is controlled by the Labour Party.[79] It relies for its control on the white working classes. These have begun at last to realise that the Labour Party does not regard their interests as part of its reason for being. Most of them have given up on voting. Some of them are attracted to the BNP.

There are, I think, no elections this year in or around Dover. But there are elections elsewhere in the country, and the ruling class plainly regards the BNP as a standing electoral and ideological threat. Its leaders are prosecuted and prosecuted again for offences that did not exist when I was a boy. Its activists are hounded from government jobs, and government workers are increasingly tendered loyalty oaths in which they are called on solemnly and sincerely to abjure the BNP and all its principles. The intention plainly is to create a society in which activists of dissident organisations cannot make a living unless they are entrepreneurs or have skills too valuable to be turned away, and in which the various organs of state are packed or terrorised into obedience to the ruling class.

---

[79] This is not true. Dover District Council is run by the Conservatives. I made a mistake. This being said, I think some of the points I am trying to make here are still true.

Look at the words used in this story to describe the BNP. It is a "hard right-wing" organisation. Its political views are "controversial." One of its leaders is "awaiting retrial on four race hate charges and was the subject of a Channel 4 documentary *Young Nazi and Proud*." We are assured that "[m]embership of the BNP is not illegal, and the party has several local councillors across the country." But the main impression any reader of the story is supposed to carry away is that the BNP is not to be tolerated beyond the bare formality of the law, and that anyone daring to be open about holding such opinions can forget about a career or even peace of mind. The language used is not neutral. It is a tool of propaganda.

On the front page of the newspaper is a picture of Miss Chamberlain. She is sat on a railway train looking back at a cameraman who has obviously just walked up and called to her. I suppose that was when she was "[c]onfronted by the *Express*"—and note the use of that hard, accusatory word. No wonder her reported comments made little sense—assuming, that is, they have been accurately reported.

Miss Chamberlain, I have little doubt, will lose her job. The Astor Theatre will then be congratulated on its stand for "tolerance" and be allowed to sink back into obscurity. And the scum who call themselves journalists and who wrote up this story—and who in other times and other places would have found employment as informers and agents of provocation—will move on to their next assignment.

But let us return to Mr Prosser, my Member of Parliament. I am never sure when I see him whether I should laugh at him or just vomit over him. He is not quite the most disgusting politician I have met. But he comes reasonably close. Forget his denunciation of the BNP as "right-wing and fascist." These words have no meaning other than to express disapproval by the ruling class. Take the word "evil." Now, I do not support the BNP—I am a libertarian: it is a white nationalist organisation. But I am not aware that the BNP has yet formed a government in this country, and that the policies of this government have given us wars of imperial aggression in the Balkans and Middle East and a police state at home. Mr Prosser has given his unwavering support to just such a government. He must take a share of responsibility for its acts. If anyone is evil, it is he. If anyone is not to be allowed near children on account of his opinions, it is he. If anyone deserves to be driven from the presence of the respectable people of his constituency, it is he.

All this being said, what is my opinion on the Chamberlain case? Do I think it right that she should keep her job—even if it may be partly funded by the taxpayers? Should she be allowed to continue teaching drama to children during the day and interviewing Nick Griffin after dark?

My answer is yes. I could take a basic libertarian position on the matter of association, and announce that her employment was purely a matter for the Astor Theatre or for anyone funding the Astor Theatre. But this basic libertarianism is not enough for me. I believe in tolerance. I can imagine a libertarian society in which no rights were violated, but where people chose to associate in mutually exclusive groups that allowed no intellectual disagreement within or difference of lifestyle. So far as there would be far less positive oppression, this kind of society would be an improvement on what we now have. I would not, however, regard it as the best of possible worlds. There is much to be said for agreeing to disagree with others and for not dwelling on points of difference.

If we had a small state, I should certainly agree with the proposition that those employed by the taxpayers should not be allowed to become activists in any political organisation. But we do not have a small state, and the millions employed directly or indirectly—often people whose legitimate career choices force them to work for the state—are at the moment required to act and speak as if they shared the opinions of the ruling class. Until we can liberate these people from state control, I think we should press for them to be allowed to express their opinions whatever these may be. People should be employed regardless of their stated opinions. They should be disciplined only when their opinions affect the quality of their work.

The standard reply to this argument is that there are some opinions so loathsome and corrupting that those holding them cannot be trusted to do their jobs. I have heard this most recently said of the lecturer Frank Ellis, suspended from his job at Leeds University for having denied the equality of the races and sexes. According to someone called Hind Hassan, treasurer of Unite Against Fascism at Leeds University and quoted in *The Guardian* on the 17th March 2006,

> This is a fight that is going to go on and on until we get rid of this man. It has gone beyond an issue of freedom of speech or academic freedom and now directly impinges on the rights of students to live and work in a

safe and tolerant environment. How can female students or those from ethnic minorities possibly get a fair educational experience? [80]

The counter-reply is that anyone who feels physically intimidated by an argument should not be at a university. Of course, the advocates of censorship have always justified themselves with talk of protecting others from harm. Those who wanted to stop people from reading about sex spoke of protecting us from depravity and corruption. The Inquisition was firm about protecting the young and ignorant from the contagion of heresy. These "anti-fascists" are no different.

I grant that children do have certain entitlements that adults do not; and if Miss Chamberlain were known to be preaching her opinions in her classes, there might be some reason for concern. But there is no evidence that this is the case. The report in *The Dover Express* goes out of its way to tell us that she is an exemplary teacher.

That being so, her opinions are a matter for her alone, and she should not be prevented from teaching drama at the Astor Theatre.

But, as said, her opinions will be taken into consideration. Her teaching days are coming to an end. Miss Chamberlain is a dissident in this country, and she and her friends had better get used to being second and even third class citizens.

---

[80] Matthew Taylor, "Students and staff protest against lecturer's race views," *The Guardian*, London, 17th March 2006.

ON CONVERSING
WITH THE BRITISH NATIONAL PARTY (2005)[81]

I wrote this article last November and then forgot about it. But the opening of the prosecution today of Nick Griffin brought it back to mind. I therefore publish it now.

I have not changed my views on how to deal with approaches from the British National Party, though the facts have since changed. The BNP Press Officer turned out to be a fool. He got into an argument with Dr Chris R. Tame over some words used in one of our news releases, and huffily demanded to be removed from all our mailing lists. It is, of course, highly convenient for us to say now that we are disliked by the BNP. But it makes no strategic sense for that Party to have decided to dislike the only political movement in this country willing to defend its rights in public and willing to speak to its officers with any degree of politeness. It also makes me wonder to what extent the BNP is controlled by the security services. A pure front organisation would surely have run at us with arms outspread, ready to enfold us in its poisonous embrace. Instead, we were told to get lost.

But here is the article as I wrote it.

On Sunday the 7th November [2004], I took a long telephone call from the Press Officer of the British National Party. This should not have surprised me. Just over a fortnight before, the Libertarian Alliance had sent out a news release deploring the fact that HSBC and Barclay's Bank had both told the BNP to take its business elsewhere, and denouncing the Government for making the first law in our history that requires political parties to register with an Electoral Commission and to have bank accounts in this country. This law makes what might otherwise be a private decision of the banks into a limitation of public debate. On the strength of that release, I did four radio discussions and gave telephone interviews to several newspapers. But I had then moved to other business

---

[81] First published on *www.seangabb.co.uk* on the 7th April 2005

Freedom of Speech in England

and was surprised to be called by an officer of the BNP, and I had to think quickly about the tone I should adopt with him.

On the basic principle, of defending the rights of BNP members to organise and publish and take part in elections, I have no difficulty. I am an officer of the Libertarian Alliance, and our policy is to defend liberty. If two men were put on trial for eating each other's excrement, we would readily go on television to defend their rights. Ours would be the only civil liberties group in the country willing to do this, I have no doubt, just as we were the only group willing last month to defend the right of some Jamaican singer—whose name escaped me even in the radio studio—to advocate the murder of homosexuals. When homosexuals were still persecuted, we defended them. We now defend their opponents when they are persecuted. As said, our policy is to defend liberty. Though our resources are too limited to do this in all cases, we do try to make some defence at the margin—that is, in those cases where the better funded but less resolute civil liberties groups are likely to think of the bad publicity involved and to bolt for cover

There is no question of our not defending the rights of BNP members. Our only concern when drafting that news release was to ask if the decision to withdraw banking services was a purely commercial response to pressure from other customers—and we believe that boycotting is part of the right to freedom of association—or if it was at least in part an attempt from a sector so regulated and cartelised as to be a private arm of the state to limit freedom of speech. We decided, taking the present state of the law into account, it was the latter, and the result can be seen on our website.

But basic principle is one thing. I had not decided—and my only excuse is that I was occupied with other matters—how to respond to an approach from the BNP. I already knew I should reject the standard response of defensive aggression. I have heard this too often. It requires a tone of exaggerated self-righteousness: "I yield to no one in my utter condemnation of these evil men. Many of my best friends are [mention some ethnic group, the more unusual the better]. I am myself half-Tibetan and one quarter Aztec..." and so on and so forth. This is degrading, and it concedes a moral superiority to the enemies of freedom of speech that they do not deserve. But while there was no doubt I should be polite, how polite should I be? After all, I do not agree with the principles and policies of the BNP. I think I adopted the right tone of polite sympathy as Mr xxx explained the raw deal his party gets from the Establishment and its tame media. But I think it would be useful for me to explain the reasons behind the tone I adopted.

If we were dealing with excrement eaters, I should be reluctant to have any dealings beyond a principled defence of their rights. There would be something so inherently nasty about their activities that no one would blame me for being rather short with them on the telephone. But it is evident to me that members of the BNP are not in this category of defended persons.

We are told the BNP is a party of national socialists, of racists and of fascists. Sometimes, these words are used as synonyms and are only uttered to add to the weight of vague denunciation. If they are thought about, however, the words are not always justly used.

A fascist, so far as I can tell, is someone who believes than an unregulated free market leads to unacceptable economic instability and unfair distributions of wealth, but who also believes that socialism is variously unworkable and immoral. He therefore believes that the state should take a more active role in national life than is allowed by the liberal philosophers: it should ensure that businesses are allowed to operate without disruption, but that the fruits are more equally shared. Of course, libertarians can reject fascism on this definition, as can radical socialists. But I fail to see how anyone else can. This has been the position of just about every mainstream political party in the civilised world during the past hundred years. The only difference between Mussolini and Lloyd George was black shirts and castor oil—and, while important, these are differences that have no bearing on the validity of the underlying analysis. For most people in this country, to denounce the BNP as fascist is as absurd as to denounce its leadership for wearing business suits.

The word "racism" has so many meanings that it has none. It can mean anything from a preference for living in communities of one's own sort to wanting to murder everyone else. Since most people come within the weaker definition and almost no one in the stronger, the word has about the same intellectual content and the same function as the growling of a dog. It simply means: "shut up, or we will turn your life into a misery." This being so, the claim that the BNP is a racist party is not worth discussing.

So far as national socialism is concerned, this is a more justified claim. A national socialist believes that the main agents in the world are not individuals but nations, and that these are defined genetically, and that each nation has its own characteristics and interests that may place it in conflict with others. Individuals are but parts of the greater nation, and stand to it as do the teeth to a comb. Since national socialism has Hegelian roots, it shares with some of the Marxists a view of knowledge in which propositions are true or false according to who is advancing them and when: therefore the often casual dismissal of "Jewish Physics" and "Jewish Political Economy." Associated with national socialism is a socialistic, protectionist approach to economic management, and some strange and intellectually indefensible theories of money and credit. And central to the ideology is the belief that a government that represents the general will of the nation should not be restrained by any legal norms or moral considerations.

On this definition, the BNP was until recently a national socialist party. Its previous leader, John Tyndal, was a disciple of Adolf Hitler, and many party members—some of them still active—belonged in their younger days to movements that plainly owed much to German national socialism.

This being said, I am not sure if the BNP now can be called national socialist. Most collectivist ideologies are absurd, but the absurdities of national socialism have been advertised so well during the past 60 years, that they are difficult to ignore. I have trouble to understand how any person of reasonable intelligence can be a national socialist. In any event, national socialism has not, and never has had, any significant electoral appeal in this country. Under its present leader, Nick Griffin, its position seems far better to be described as white nationalist. This is an ideology that regards nations—defined according to common appearance, though perhaps also to other criteria—as important, and insists that each nation so far as possible should have its own territory, and should keep to its own national ways. In a loose sense, this is a position shared by most people, but it has, over the past few decades, been refined into a distinctive ideology; and perhaps its most intellectually coherent expression can be found in the group of writers assembled around Jared Taylor, the editor of *American Renaissance*.

There are points of agreement between white nationalism and national socialism. But this does not justify conflating the two. After all, there are points of agreement between Trotskyism and syndicalism—just as there are between typhus and the bubonic plague—but it is generally seen as more useful to focus on the points of difference. White nationalists may believe in some degree of tariff protection, but do not necessarily share

On Conversing with the BNP

the more socialistic views of the national socialists—especially if they are members of a nation within which market exchange is part of the culture. They also do not necessarily share the anti-semitism of the national socialists. Perhaps they dislike those Jews who think of themselves as expatriate Israelis. But they do not dislike Jews for purely genetic reasons, and usually accept the assimilated as potentially valuable members of the white race. Indeed, *American Renaissance* has Jewish contributors; and the BNP recently put up a Jewish candidate for election. Most importantly, perhaps, white nationalists accept at least the principle of working within legal norms that may be highly liberal—even if they do not believe in applying those norms outside their own racial grouping.

As with any political movement that is changing its ideology, there are firm advocates of both old and new, and the majority of members who hold to a shifting and often inconsistent mixture of both. See, for example, the Labour Party, which moved in the late 1980s from various kinds of socialism to a politically correct social democracy: it is the party of Tony Blair, of Gordon Brown and of Jeremy Corbyn. Look at the old Liberal Party: well into the 1950s—long after it had become a party of social democracy—it still included a few classical liberals. The BNP is in much the same position. The leadership is increasingly drawn to white nationalism, but the older activists retain more than a tinge of national socialism. The leaders themselves may have once been national socialists, but are no longer—just as half the present Ministers seem once to have been radical socialists. Because the BNP is a persecuted movement, and therefore finds it more than usually difficult to find new activists, it is reasonable to expect this ideological divide to continue for at least the next decade. Even so, I am not sure that it is appropriate, on the basis of some of its older activists—or even on what may remain the esoteric doctrines of the leadership—to define the BNP as national socialist.

I will emphasise that the views of the BNP do not in the least influence the willingness of the Libertarian Alliance to defend its rights to organise and operate. We defend the right of BNP members to freedom of speech and association. But the nature of these views does affect how polite we feel we ought to be to members of the BNP. National socialism has its place within a collectivist spectrum that inspired the murder of perhaps a hundred million people in the last century. National socialists, in our view, are as infamous as Trotskyites, Stalinists, Maoists, and others of that kind. Taken together, they stand lower in our regard than they

Freedom of Speech in England

hypothetical excrement eaters mentioned above—who only want to inflict their nastiness on themselves and each other.

But, while I am not a white nationalist, I see no reason whatever to regard white nationalists as political lepers. I loathe and abhor the Labour Party, both as it used to be and as it has now become. I have little time for the Conservative Party. But I have close friends in both these parties; and, unless I have a specific reason not to be, I am generally polite to other activists and Members of Parliament. I do not see why a party of white nationalists should be treated any differently.

This being said, there are two considerations that affect my response to approaches from the BNP. The first is that the BNP is a persecuted movement. It cannot rent public facilities. It cannot open bank accounts in this country. Election laws are being drafted or redrafted to prevent it from winning seats on representative bodies. If it does manage to win seats in local administration, conventions are changed to deny it any administrative power. Its members either are hounded informally from their jobs and homes, or are subject to formal pressures. And persecution is not confined to party members, but spreads in some vague way to those who associate with them. I have some firmness of mind—after all, I am willing to argue for freedom when others find it convenient to look the other way. But I am not willing to put myself in a position where I cannot find work and where my friends are frightened to be seen in public with me. Had I been alive and active in the early twentieth century, I am sure I would have spoken out against the persecution of homosexuals. But would I have shared a platform with Edward Carpenter? Would I have posed beside John Gielgud just after his cottaging conviction? I like to think that I would, but do not believe I would. There is in such matters both a primary and a secondary persecution; and though far less damaging than the first, I have no wish to risk the second.

There are limits to my timidity. Last year, I took part in a radio programme that included Tony Martin, and I have on my website photographs of the two of us in friendly conversation. Now that Mr Martin has joined the BNP, I have not the slightest intention of taking those photographs down. Equally, if one of my closest friends were to join the BNP, I would make a point of not altering my personal behaviour towards him. But while I will not choose my friends or alter my past according to the political shifts of others, I will not put myself with full prior knowledge into a position of risk.

The second consideration is that the BNP has never been a normal political movement. There are excellent reasons to believe it is a creature of the security services. I cannot—or will not—give my reasons. But I have no doubt that most of those prominent within the BNP are controlled by the security services. Its purpose is to attract support that might otherwise go to genuine white nationalist movements—and to neutralise that support by ensuring that advances are never followed through. Its purpose is also to taint whole bodies of analysis and policy so that they can be dismissed by the Establishment without the trouble of a refutation. Thus most discussion of how immigration is changing the demographic profile of this country remains dangerous because anyone who speaks about it too openly will be smeared as a fellow traveller of the BNP. Though without success, a similar tactic has been used against Euroscepticism. Whether or not it is a front organisation has no bearing on the civil and political liberties of its members. But it does have a bearing—taken together with the risk of secondary persecution—on my willingness to associate myself in any capacity with the BNP.

So I have explained the response that I have made and will continue to make to approaches from the BNP. I will not just defend the rights of BNP members, but will also be polite to its officers. Anyone who thinks this is an admission to be used against me is either stupid or malevolent. I have given my reasons.

More on the
Persecution of the BNP (2007)[82]

One of my duties as Director of the Libertarian Alliance is to defend the right to free expression of people whose views I may not share. I do not perform this duty as often or as effectively as I might wish. But I begin the new year with another of my comments on the persecution of the British National Party.

Just before last Christmas, a journalist called Ian Cobain published a series of articles in *The Guardian* newspaper, revealing how he had joined the BNP and been made its Central London Organiser. In this capacity, he got hold of the Party's membership list. His articles were essentially a listing of names of middle class members. Further news reports in the same newspaper and in others detailed the actual and suggested persecution of these members.

The most widely discussed member has been Simone Clarke, a leading dancer at the English National Ballet. She was quoted by Mr Cobain as saying that immigration "has really got out of hand." The ENB is a body funded by the taxpayers, and it has a duty under the Race Relations Act 2000 to "promote good race relations."[83] The funding body, Arts Council England, insists that funded "organisations have to make sure that they promote cultural diversity as a clear and central part of all their work."[84]

Not surprisingly, there have been calls for her to be sacked. Lee Jasper, Equalities Director for the Mayor of London and Chairman of the National Assembly Against Racism, said:

> The ENB must seriously consider whether having such a vociferous member of an avowedly racist party in such a prominent role is compatible with the ethics of its organisation. I seriously doubt that it is

---

[82] Published on *www.seangabb.co.uk* on the 3rd January 2007.

[83] Ian Cobain, "The Guardian journalist who became central London organiser for the BNP," *The Guardian*, London, 21st December 2006.

[84] *www.artscouncil.org.uk/documents/information/php48fkTn.doc*

More on the Persecution of the BNP

and that should lead to her position being immediately reviewed. I think she should be sacked.[85]

He called on funders and David Lammy, the Arts Minister, to intervene.

Inayat Bunglawala, of the Muslim Council of Britain, said people had a right to their private political views but added:

> This will taint the ENB in the eyes of many minority communities. Questions need to be asked about how someone in that position can be allowed to abuse that position to promote the BNP."[86]

I could move to my analysis of the agenda behind Mr Cobain's articles. But I cannot resist a brief digression on Mr Bunglawala. He is treated in the coverage of this story as if he were a political moderate, righteously shocked at the "political extremism" of the BNP. In fact, his own opinions appear quite as alarming as anything alleged against the BNP.

Take his statement that people have a right to their *private* political views. That may be the case in some benevolent oriental despotism. In England, it has long been accepted that we have a right to express our political views *in public*. Such, at least, has always been my understanding.

Turning to his comments on the ENB, it is worth asking what possible further taint he thinks the organisation can receive through its association with Miss Clarke. He appears to believe that western classical music is a sinful indulgence, and that listening to it is inconsistent with Islam. He makes a point of rejecting the more purist Islamic position, that

> Listening to music and singing is a sin and cause for the sickening and weakening of the heart. The majority of the scholars of the Salaf are unanimous that listening to music and singing and using musical instruments is Haram (prohibited). [87]

He says instead that:

> We accept music but would frown on disco-going, or concerts where alcohol is served or where there is unrestricted mixing of the sexes. That

---

[85] Hugh Muir, "BNP ballerina defies rising clamour to sack her," *The Guardian*, London, 1st January 2007.

[86] *ibid.*

[87] Islam Singing and Music Are Forbidden: wn.com/Islam_Singing_and_Music_are_Forbidden

would be opposed by Islamic scholars.[88]

But where is the difference? While in Bratislava last month, I attended a performance of *La Traviata*. The plot centres on the relationship between an unmarried man and a high class prostitute. There was shameless mingling of the sexes in the audience. There was alcohol served in the intervals. During Act 2, Scene 2, the ballerinas showed their legs most immodestly and contorted their bodies in ways that might have given Mr Bunglawala a seizure.

He says he accepts music. Has he ever seen *The Rite of Spring*? Is he aware of the double orgasm portrayed in the Overture to *Don Giovanni*? Does he know the score of *Tristan und Isolde*? Would he recommend Moslems to attend any of these works? So long as she refrains from lecturing the audience between pirouettes, does it add to the infamy of a performance if Miss Clarke holds opinions of which he disapproves?

But enough of Mr Bunglawala. I turn to the main agenda.

We have in this country a ruling class committed to political, economic and social globalisation. While some parts of this are consistent with libertarianism, others are not. Much of the consequent association of peoples takes place in a market systematically rigged by taxes and regulations. Much is nakedly coerced through equal opportunity laws and censorship. But whatever libertarians might think of what is going on, large and increasing numbers of people dislike it all.

Since both main political parties are agreed, opponents have a choice between not voting at all and voting for one of the smaller parties. Many are voting for the BNP. There is a chance that many who do not vote will also vote BNP once it can prove that it is a credible political force. Therefore, the BNP must be destroyed.

The gentler forms of destruction involve lies. Undoubtedly, the BNP grew out of a national socialist movement. But it does not appear now to be a national socialist organisation. So far as I can tell from its website, the BNP believes in a mixed economy welfare state, with some regard for traditional civil liberties. It also believes that the alleged benefits of this should be largely reserved for English-speaking white people. This is not something that I find particularly attractive. Nor however is it the same as wanting a totalitarian police state plus gas chambers.

---

[88] Stephen Moss, "The hills are alive," *The Guardian*, London, 15th November 2001.

More on the Persecution of the BNP

Since lying about the BNP does not work very well in the age of the Internet, the gentler forms of destruction are being supplemented by stronger. Its leader has just been acquitted after a trial for speech crimes that did not exist when I was a boy. Its known members are losing their jobs in public bodies up and down the country. It has trouble getting its material printed. Banks are being persuaded to close its accounts. The legal machinery is in place to deny it access to the ballot in elections.

Mr Cobain's articles must be seen as part of this attempted destruction of a political party. Let it become known that middle class supporters will be named and have their careers destroyed, and party membership will not proceed far beyond the working classes. Let it be made effectively impossible for any middle class person to stand as a BNP candidate, and the only candidates will be criminals and fools, who can then be held up as a reason not to vote BNP.

Much of this would be happening if there were a Conservative Government. But the intensity of the persecution faced by the BNP is peculiar to Labour. There has been a strain of antinomianism in our politics since 1997 not seen in centuries. From Tony Blair down, the Ministers believe passionately that they can and therefore must turn England into some kind of multicultural love feast. Their vision of a transformed England is not very clear. But, as with an impressionist painting, vagueness of detail is compensated by vividness of colour.

These people cannot imagine that anyone of good will could fail to believe as they do. Therefore, all opposition is evil, and may rightly be put down without regard for traditional norms of right and justice and common decency. See, as an example of this, how Peter Hain defends as a Minister police state measures that he used to condemn when used by the South African Government.[89] To the Saints of New Labour, all things are lawful.

It helps that most of these people used to be Marxists. They no longer seem to believe in the positive doctrines of Marxism, but they retain its assumption that the traditional norms are mere "bourgeois legality."

We can, therefore, look forward to much more of this. Sooner or later, our ruling class will shut down all electoral dissent. The only possible opposition will then be on the streets.

---

[89] This being house arrest: *en.wikipedia.org/wiki/Peter_Hain*

Freedom of Speech in England

Now, I am able to say this from a position of safety. Neither I nor the Libertarian Alliance expect to suffer in any measurable degree from this shutting down of debate. We live in a potemkin democracy, where only limited diversity of opinion is tolerated. But even so, there must be some opposition.

I am fortunate enough to find myself in the licensed opposition. I face no official discrimination that I can see. I am allowed to work in state universities. I am allowed regular appearances in the media. I am not obviously under surveillance. This may be because our ruling class does not regard libertarians as much of a threat. It may be because someone outside the ruling class has to be tolerated, for the sake of keeping up the pretence of liberal democracy. Whatever the reason, we do not operate under any of the disadvantages that the real dissidents of the BNP must take as facts of life.

This imposes a duty on me and my friends to speak up in defence of the dissidents. Unlike the other "rights" organisations, we believe in freedom of speech with no exceptions. We do not enquire into the substance of a person's views before defending his right to express them.

We denounce the persecution of the BNP. Though I do not expect them to pay any attention, I call on Liberty and the Conservative Party to do likewise.

THE BRITISH STATE V THE BNP: THE POST-MODERN TYRANNY OF "HUMAN RIGHTS" (2009)[90]

On Monday the 24th August 2009, the British Equality and Human Rights Commission (EHRC) began legal proceedings against the British National Party (BNP). Its cause of action is that the BNP restricts membership to white people. This is said to be illegal under the Race Relations Act 1976 as amended in 2000. If successful, the court action will force the BNP to open its membership to all applicants regardless of their colour.

This is a politically-motivated prosecution. The BNP has long upset the people who now rule Britain. Its denunciations of mass-immigration and of multiculturalism disrupt what would otherwise be an almost smooth wall of praise—or at least of caution—by the other parties. Despite universal condemnation in the media, it has made considerable gains during the past few years in local elections, and managed to win two seats in June this year in the European Parliament. It may win a seat in the British Parliament at the next general election. Stopping the BNP is high on the agenda of the powers that be.

This being said, shutting down a political party simply because it dissents from the established multicultural faith is not something that is yet done in Britain. It is too open an attack on freedom of speech. It may also be illegal under the Human Rights Act 1998, which enacts the European Convention on Human Rights into British law. And so the party is to be ruined partly by the costs of legal action, and partly by the effects of losing the legal action.

These effects have been clearly spelled out by some of the BNP's enemies. According to the Blog of Operation Black Vote,

> Nic Careem, a former Labour activist from Camden in north London, who is now with the Conservatives, said he originally argued that black

---

[90] First published on *www.vdare.com* on the 31st August 2009. My thanks to Peter Brimelow for his permission to republish it here.

and Asian people should join the BNP en mass [sic] to cause chaos and expose the extent of racism inside the party of Nick Griffin. [91]

In other words, the BNP is to be flooded with non-whites, who will then use further legal action—assuming the internal structures of the party are insufficient—to destroy it.

This attack on the BNP is abhorrent for a number of reasons.

First, it is indirectly an attack on freedom of speech. We are endlessly told nowadays that this does not involve the right to preach hatred and "intolerance." But it does. Freedom of speech means the right to say anything at all on any public issue, and to make any recommendation on what the law should be. I was born into a country where this understanding was broadly accepted. I live now in a country where it is not. Simon Woolley of Operation Black Vote dismisses freedom of speech as an "almost sacred cow." [92] He even appeals for support to the majesty of the British Constitution:

> Over centuries our unwritten constitution has given us a framework for our democracy. From Magna Carta to the Race Relations (Amendment) Act 2000, our democracy has evolved to reflect our changing times. This framework gives us a democracy which, for all its limitations, seeks to balance individual freedoms with fairness and tolerance. [93]

In the technical sense, he may be right. Being unwritten, the British Constitution is whatever the authorities decide it to be. But his claim is irrelevant. A constitution does not legitimise oppression. Rather, it is legitimate so far as it protects rights. If the British Constitution no longer guarantees freedom of speech, so much the worse for the Constitution.

Second, as said, the authorities are frightened to make a direct attack on freedom of speech. Instead, they are relying on laws that abolish freedom of association. But this is barely less important within the liberal tradition than freedom of speech. The two rights complement each other. Freedom of speech is the right to say anything. Freedom of association involves the right to propagate what is said. It means the right of people

---

[91] "We should have challenged the BNP years ago," 25th August 2009: *operationblackvote.wordpress.com/2009/08/25/we-should-have-challenge-the-bnp-years-ago/*

[92] "Bringing the BNP to book," 25th August 2009: *operationblackvote.wordpress.com/2009/08/25/bringing-the-bnp-to-book/*

[93] *Ibid.*

The Post-Modern Tyranny of "Human Rights"

to come together for any purpose that does not involve aggression against others.

Obviously, it also means the right *not* to associate. Laws imposing equal access to employment, or paid services, or membership of private associations, are not an extension of rights, but a denial of rights. By forcing people to associate with persons whom they would otherwise reject, anti-discrimination laws are a form of coerced association. They also allow dissident organisations to be taken over and destroyed.

Third, if the form of the attack is hypocritical, so is the substance. The BNP is not the only organisation that seeks to confine its membership to members of a particular race. But it is the only organisation the EHRC is taking to court. The Lincolnshire Black Police Association, for example, declares on its website—rather, it declares on its section of the official web site of the Lincolnshire Police Force—that

> Membership applications for the LBPA are invited from everybody. Full Membership is available to all Black Minority Ethnic staff of the Lincolnshire Police. Associate Membership is open to ALL members of the Lincolnshire Police and outside agencies who wish to support the work of the LBPA. [94]

I am told that these confessions of racial discrimination are being hurriedly taken down from the Internet. However, the BNP has published a selection of screen shots from the Lincolnshire and other branches of the Black Police Association.[95] The EHRC has so far refused even to acknowledge complaints of this racial discrimination.

And even if the Black Police Association should take down the offending words and open its full membership to all, there is no chance of its being flooded by hostile whites. There are no white equivalents of Operation Black Vote or other ethnic advocacy groups. Any that did form would soon be prosecuted or harassed out of existence. Any individual whites who joined would themselves be evangelists of the multicultural faith. If not, they would be chased out with violence or threats of violence that the Police would do nothing to investigate.

---

[94] It says this no longer (December 2011)! But it once said it here: *www.lincs.police.uk/index.asp?locID=184&docID=106*

[95] *bnp.org.uk/2009/08/exposed-the-%e2%80%9cblacks-only%e2%80%9d-police-association-that-the-cehr-ignores/*

Freedom of Speech in England

Fourth, it is at least interesting to see how the language of rights has been perverted into a cover for oppression. The Equality and Human Rights Commission promotes equality by discriminating against whites, and protects human rights by attacking freedom of association as a means of neutering freedom of speech. It is also interesting that the EHRC Commissioner overseeing the BNP prosecution is John Wadham. He was once Director of Liberty, which is supposed to be the main independent guardian in this country of civil and political rights. At a public meeting in 2001, I accused Mr Wadham of not caring about the liberties of anyone perceived to be on the political "right." This sent him into a rhetorical frenzy. A few weeks later, I felt almost guilty at how roughly I had treated him when I read this in a letter of his to *The Daily Telegraph*:

> [H]uman rights are primarily about limiting the power of the central state in its dealing with the individual citizen. [96]

According to the accounts of the body that the EHRC replaced, Mr Wadham's salary in the year to the 31st March 2008 was £78,548.[97] I will limit my comments on this fact to observing that his salary—and it has probably risen by a third in the past 18 months—is at least three times his probable worth in any market-based employment.

By way of a conclusion, I feel I ought to give my opinion on the BNP. This is that I fear its success. The next Conservative Government will fail to reverse the disasters that Labour has brought on the country. This is because the Conservatives do not even intend to try for a counter-revolution. When the failure has become manifest, people will turn to the only alternative party that has forthrightly denounced the Labour revolution and has an existing electoral base. This will be the BNP. I fear that the BNP will, by default, become the only viable champion of counter-revolution.

Now, I am not frightened that the BNP is a party of national socialists, and that its leaders are counting the days till they can rip off their business suits, to show the black and red uniforms beneath. Under its present leader, Nick Griffin, the BNP has become a white nationalist party. The party believes in the expulsion of illegal immigrants, and in some voluntary repatriation of non-whites who are legally here, and in dismantling the equal opportunities police state from which people like

---

[96] John Wadham, letter, "Human rights part of Tory tradition," *The Daily Telegraph*, London, 26th March 2001.

[97] *www.official-documents.gov.uk/document/hc0809/hc06/0632/0632.pdf*

The Post-Modern Tyranny of "Human Rights"

Mr Wadham benefit. Other than this, a BNP Government might easily show more respect for the forms of a liberal constitution than Labour has—after all, this would not be difficult.

The problem is that the BNP and much of its leading personnel *used to be* national socialists. There are too many published statements in praise of Hitler or denouncing the Jews. Of course, people change their opinions over time. Middle aged men are not necessarily to be judged on what they said or wrote in their late teens. That excuse has been made and accepted for the Ministers in the Labour Government. Many of these in their younger days were Trotskyite street bullies. Peter Mandelson, who is effectively deputy Prime Minister, joined the Young Communist League three years after the Soviet invasion of Czechoslovakia, and used to sell the Communist *Morning Star*. John Reid, who was a Home Secretary in the Blair Government, was a member of the Communist Party in his late twenties, and was noted for his admiration of Josef Stalin. It would be easy to fill an article with the disreputable pasts of those who have ruled this country since 1997. If there were any fairness in politics, they would be regarded as no less disreputable than the leaders of the BNP.

But there is no fairness in politics. A man can deny the Soviet holocaust—or even admit that it happened but try to justify it—and remain in good standing with the media and educational establishment. The slightest whisper of approval for the lesser horrors of national socialism, and a man is tainted for life. This is unfair, but it is a fact that must be accepted. I can easily imagine how the BNP might replace the useless Conservatives as main opponents to what has been done to this country. I can also imagine how the movement then led by the BNP might be smeared and discredited out of existence.

Even so, if I can have no longing for a BNP breakthrough at the next but one general election, neither can I regard the legal proceedings against it as other than a classic illustration of how to run a post-modern tyranny. The British State has no Gestapo, no KGB. Why does it need one when it has the Equality and Human Rights Commission?

NEWS FROM THE BRITISH POLICE STATE: EQUALITY BY DECREE! (2010)[98]

At the moment in Britain, the Government's Equalities Bill is completing its progress through Parliament. The purpose of the Bill is to bring all the various "equality" laws made since 1965—race, sex, sexual preference, age-based, religious, etc—within a single statute, and to enable a single scheme of enforcement. It also tightens these laws so that such discrimination as has continued to exist will be made illegal.

The exact meaning of any proposed law is hard to judge in advance. We need to see the final Act of Parliament. We need to see the hundreds of pages of regulations that it enables through its delegated legislation sections. We need to see how it will be enforced by the authorities, and how the courts will rule on its interpretation. But the law as it stands is already reasonably clear. It is, for example, illegal for a Jewish school not to accept gentile children. It is illegal for a Christian hotelier to refuse to let two homosexuals share a bed together. It is illegal for an employer to exclude job candidates who belong to a group of which he might—for whatever reason—disapprove, or to confine recruitment within those groups of which he does approve. The same applies to landlords. It is also illegal for the British National Party to confine its membership to those it regards as indigenous to the British Isles.

In a recent defeat in the House of Lords, the Government will not be able to force religious schools to employ teachers who are outside of or hostile to their religious values. But this defeat may be reversed when the Bill returns to the Commons. Or it may be reversed by separate legislation. As said, a law cannot be exactly understood until it is in force. Even so, the Equalities Bill must be regarded as one of the most important measures in the consolidation of the British police state.

---

[98] First published on *www.vdare.com* on the 27th January 2010. My thanks to Peter Brimelow for his permission to republish it here.

Equality by Decree

The problem with opposing this sort of law is that opponents can be written off as opposed to equality in general, or even as bigots. This is, however, an illegitimate tactic. As with freedom, everyone nowadays believes in equality. The real question is what is meant by equality.

According to the mainstream liberal tradition, as it runs through Locke, Hume, Mill and Hayek, everyone has—or should be regarded as having—an equal right to his life, liberty and property. This means that everyone should be equal before the law. Unless she agrees in advance, a married woman should not lose the right to own property. A Roman Catholic should not be prohibited from inheriting under his father's will. An atheist or Jew should not be denied justice because he will not swear as a witness on the New Testament. Everyone should have the same right of access to the courts. Everyone should have the same rights to freedom of thought and speech and faith, and to freedom of association, and to freedom from arbitrary fine or imprisonment.

And that is it. The mainstream liberal tradition does not insist that everyone should have the same right to a job, or residential letting, or service in a restaurant or hotel. No one should have the right to be loved or accepted by others. If the owner of a business puts a note in his window advertising that he will not deal with Jews or homosexuals or the disabled, that is his right. As a liberal, I would regard this kind of announcement with distaste, and I might refuse, because of it, to deal with that business. But that is the limit of proper disapproval. It is not a matter for interference by the authorities.

Now, I have argued so far as if I assumed that the projectors of the Equalities Bill were people of good intentions but limited understanding. I do not assume this for a moment. The people who rule my country are best described as evil. They have not been led astray by bad ideas. Rather, they are bad people who choose bad ideologies to justify their behaviour.

There are ideologies of the left—mutualism, for example, or Georgism, or syndicalism—that may often be silly or impracticable, but that are perfectly consistent with the dignity and independence of ordinary people. These are not ideologies, however, of which those who rule us have ever taken the smallest notice. These people began as state socialists. When this became electorally embarrassing, they switched to politically correct multiculturalism. Now this too is becoming an embarrassment, they are moving towards totalitarian environmentalism. Whether in local or in national government, their proclaimed ideologies have never prevented them from working smoothly with multinational big business, or with unaccountable multinational governing bodies.

It is reasonable to assume that, with these people, ideas are nothing more than a series of justifications for building a social and economic and political order within which they and theirs can have great wealth and unchallengeable power. Their object has been to deactivate all the mechanisms that once existed in this country for holding its rulers accountable to the ruled.

And that is what they have been doing since the Labour Party won the 1997 election. To a degree that foreigners do not often realise, Britain has, during the past thirteen years, been through a revolution. This has been brought about by the Government and by its collaborators in the mainstream media, in the administration, and in big business. They have swept away the constitutional settlement of the seventeenth century. Our Ancient Constitution may have struck outsiders as a gigantic fancy dress ball. But it covered a serious and very important fact. This was an imperfect acceptance of Colonel Rainsborough's claim that "the poorest he that is in England hath a life to live as the greatest he." It allowed this country to be at once highly conservative in its institutions and, at the same time, free.

This has gone. Since 1997, we have had four thousand new criminal offences created—no one knows what they all are, but many deal with censorship of speech and publication. They are usually enforced by a summary—and often arbitrary and even corrupt—process. The traditional courts and their procedure have also been transformed, so that no one whose legal education ended before 1997 has the faintest idea of how to enforce his rights. We have been made formally subject to the European Union. The country has been deliberately flooded with immigrants.[99] And the purpose of mass immigration has been to break up the solidarity of the ruled.

I was born in a free country. People could speak as they pleased and live without constant supervision. If a policeman knocked on my parents' front door, their only worry was that he might have bad news. I live in a police state. If I am accused of so much as dropping a sweet wrapper on the ground, I can be arrested and taken to a police station. There, I shall have my fingerprints and a DNA sample taken. Even if I am released

---

[99] *news.sky.com/skynews/Home/Politics/Ex-Government-Adviser-Andrew-Neather-Says-Mass-Immigration-To-UK-Was-Deliberate/Article/200910415414170*

Equality by Decree

without charge, these records will be kept indefinitely. They will also be shared with several dozen foreign governments, who often regard presence on a DNA database as evidence of a criminal record. The natural response is that sensible men do all that is needed to avoid any police attention. That means prompt obedience to commands that may have no legal basis. And what is that but a police state?

I live in a country where, if I want a meeting with someone strongly disliked by the authorities, I must arrange to meet in secret—where, if I want to discuss certain topics in public, I must drop my voice to avoid being overheard by paid informers.

The Equalities Bill is simply another step in the consolidation of this new order of things. It is a bribe to those groups whose electoral support is needed to keep the Government in power. It is one more excuse for making victims of known dissidents. Above all, it is another message sent out to all of who is boss, and who must at all times be obeyed on threat of deliberately expensive and biased legal process.

The only equality the rulers of my country are working towards is equal fear of them and what they can do to us.

Putting a Nail in the Fuse Box:
The Persecution of
the British National Party (2010)[100]

For those who may be unaware of it, the British National Party is what its name says it is. It opposes mass-immigration and the associated political correctness and attacks on freedom of speech and association. It also opposes British membership of the European Union and British involvement in wars of military aggression that do nothing to secure the peace and prosperity of the British people. It is also contemptuous of the claims about man-made climate change that are an excuse for the massive enrichment of ruling classes everywhere.

Not surprisingly, the BNP is not popular with the British ruling class. This has been hard at work for at least two generations on destroying a constitution that, since the high middle ages, had been uniquely effective at restraining power. It is a ruling class that rejoices in having put common law protections through a shredding machine, and in alienating sovereignty to a mass of foreign and even unknown organisations, to the point where democracy has become a joke, and in sponsoring the mass-immigration needed to reduce working class living standards and to justify totalitarian witch-hunts.

Yes, not surprisingly, the BNP is a witch that must be hunted. It is described as a "racist" party, and its members as violent and even psychopathic criminals. Its leader, Nick Griffin, is remarkable for his ability to assemble softly-spoken persons of quality into something like a baying mob.

To describe all the ways in which the Mr Griffin and his party are persecuted would take an essay that was also a dissertation on the growth of the British police state. I have not the space to write such an essay. Therefore, I will look at the two chief current persecutions.

---

[100] First published on *www.vdare.com* on the 9th November 2010. My thanks to Peter Brimelow for his permission to republish it here.

Putting a Nail in the Fuse Box

The first was announced on Tuesday the 2nd November 2010, when Michael Gove, the Secretary of State for Education told *The Guardian* newspaper that he would allow headmasters of state schools to dismiss any teachers known to be members of the BNP. The ostensible reason for this is that members of the BNP cannot be trusted not to preach "hatred" in the classroom. Mr Gove said:

> I don't believe that membership of the BNP is compatible with being a teacher. One of the things I plan to do is to allow headteachers and governing bodies the powers and confidence to be able to dismiss teachers engaging in extremist activity. [101]

He did add that this permission to dismiss would also cover members of other "extremist" organisations. However, it is to be doubted if radical Moslems and members of Trotskyite groups will be at risk of losing their jobs. There are too many of them in teaching, and they are too well-organised and too well-connected. The permission might eventually be extended to religious Jews and Christians who refuse to celebrate the rich diversity of sexual orientations that is part of our established faith in England. Or it might not. But the permission will be ruthlessly used to seek out and remove all schoolteachers who are, or who might have been, members of the BNP.

The second persecution has been under way for a couple of years. There is in England a taxpayer-funded body called the Equality and Human Rights Commission.[102] This was set up under the Equality Act 2006, and it supposedly exists to ensure that people are treated fairly and have their rights respected. One of its main functions has been to sue the BNP to the verge of bankruptcy in the name of human rights.

In August 2009, the Commission began proceedings against the BNP under sections 24 and 25(5) of the Equality Act, on the grounds that BNP membership was confined to natives of the British Isles and white foreigners. Apparently, it was a violation of the Race Relations Act 1976 (as amended) that non-whites were not allowed to join a party committed to keeping Britain predominantly white. Since then, the Commission has been lavishing the taxpayers' money on an action that is supposed to vindicate the right of non-whites to join the BNP—a questionable cause of action, bearing in mind that few non-whites can really be aching to join an organisation like the BNP, and bearing in mind that the British

---

[101] *www.guardian.co.uk/education/2010/nov/02/bnp-members-barred-teaching*

[102] *www.equalityhumanrights.com/*

Freedom of Speech in England

State overall has been running the biggest budget deficit in the civilised world.

But vindicating abstract rights has not been the purpose of the action. Its real purpose has been to shut down the BNP. The legal proceedings could achieve this in three ways:

First, the BNP might lose and be compelled to admit large numbers of non-white members. These could then exploit its internal structures or take further legal action until there was no more BNP.

Second, the BNP might lose and then be sued again for breach of the final order. This could result in forfeiture of all party assets and the jailing of Mr Griffin.

Third, win or lose, the BNP might be forced into bankruptcy by the costs of defending an action that had unlimited funding.

This real purpose became absolutely clear in the March of 2010, when the BNP did change its rules to admit non-whites, and the Commission immediately moved to the second option in its strategy for destruction. The party imposed two conditions on new members to prevent flooding attempts. First, prospective members should be visited at home, to see if they were suitable for membership. Second, all members should declare support for the "continued creation, fostering, maintenance and existence" of an indigenous British race, and should support action towards "stemming and reversing" immigration. The Commission argued that these conditions amounted to "indirect racial discrimination."

The Commission won this round. On the 12th March 2010, a Judge outlawed the requirement for home visits, saying that this might lead to intimidation—though admitting that there was no evidence it ever had. He also outlawed the requirement to declare support for party principle and policy. He said:

> I hold that the BNP are likely to commit unlawful acts of discrimination within section 1b Race Relations Act 1976 in the terms on which they are prepared to admit persons to membership under the 12th addition of their constitution. [103]

The reason for this, the Judge went on, was that no non-white person could support these policies without compromising his "personal sense

---

[103] www.manchestereveningnews.co.uk/news/s/1200216_new_bnp_membership_rules_judged_to_be_biased

of self-worth and dignity as a member of their racial group." And so the BNP changed its membership rules again, now accepting members regardless of whether they agreed with its policies.

However, these conditions for membership were only suspended by the BNP, not removed. And so the Commission went to court again, this time arguing that the BNP was in contempt for not complying in full with the earlier judgment.

The hearing took place in London on the 8th and 9th November 2010. Since judgment was reserved, we do not yet know whether BNP assets will be seized and whether nick Griffin will be sent to prison. We can, however, be sure that, if it turns out to have lost, the Commission will find some other grounds of continuing its taxpayer-funded vendetta against the BNP. How much more of this the BNP can take before it goes bankrupt is hard to say. As of August 2010, the BNP was said to be £500,000 in debt[104]. This is about a quarter of its annual income. Much of this debt appears to have been run up in legal costs.

Every time I write one of these articles about the persecution of the BNP, I get several dozen e-mails from people who claim that the party really is a national socialist organisation, and that its recent conversion, under Nick Griffin, is a convenient lie. I find this an irrelevant claim. I happen to believe that the BNP *is* a white nationalist organisation. Even if it were not, though—even if the BNP leadership really did believe that non-whites were less than human and that the holocaust never happened, but should have, the rights and wrongs of this case would be unchanged.

It is unfair to treat people in this manner. What has been done, and is being done, to the BNP is oppressive. It is not the sort of thing that happens in a functioning liberal democracy. In a liberal democracy, people have an unquestioned right to say whatever they please on public issues—and they do not suffer even official discrimination, let alone legal harassment. In a liberal democracy, they have an unquestioned right to associate or not with whomever they please—and are not subject to administrative and legal bullying about "inclusiveness" and the unacceptability of "hate." The fact that BNP members and the party itself are victims of state harassment—and, as said, there is much more than the two instances just given—indicates just how much England has moved towards totalitarianism.

---

[104] *www.ukdebate.co.uk/forums/index.php?topic=14265.0*

Freedom of Speech in England

I go further. If Nick Griffin and the BNP were openly avowed followers of Adolf Hitler, and if they met together in public to listen to the webcasts of Harold Covington, they would probably be more left alone than they are. They are persecuted for their opinions on race and immigration. But they are persecuted still more because of all else they oppose or stand for. For all it did badly in the elections of May 2010, the BNP remains the one possible voice for working class dissent from the established order of things. Though with a sneer on its collective face, and a nod and a wink to its politicised police and judges, the British ruling class can live with a party that complains about race and immigration. It will ruthlessly smash a party that complains about this and everything else.

And though unfair in itself, what is being done to the BNP should make any reasonable man worried about the future of England. Anyone who looks at the various manifestos and pronouncements of the BNP will see a party that claims to believe—and possibly does believe—in freedom of speech and association, in trial by jury, and generally in constitutional government as this has always been understood in England. It does not even advocate compulsory repatriation of those non-whites who are legally here. Whatever it may or may not believe in private, the BNP leadership is very distant in what it says from the Hitler-loving caricatures shown in the mainstream media.

But destroy the BNP, and the result will not be a vacuum. Other movements will emerge. These will be less interested in organising to win elections and debates than in arguing their case on the streets. Already, there is an English Defence League that has no apparent interest in electoral politics. This is almost certainly less thuggish than the ruling class and the mainstream media claim it to be. Equally, though, it is less constitutional in its aims and methods than the BNP. And the English Defence League may be only the beginning of the next stage in working class dissent from the established order of things.

Until modern trip switches became the norm, household wiring in England was protected from overheating by wired fuses. Each ceramic fuse contained about an inch and a half of wire to a stated ampage. This connected power as it came into a property to one ring circuit. Any power surge or appliance failure would result in immediate burning out of the fuse. The fuses were deliberately the weakest point in the whole wiring system. One reason they have now been replaced with trip switches is because many people were in the habit of replacing fuse wires with nails. This meant that fuses never blew—instead, houses burned down.

Putting a Nail in the Fuse Box

What the British State is doing to the BNP is the political equivalent of sticking a nail in the fuse box. The destruction of the BNP will buy a few more years of life for the politically correct fantasy of England as a country of enlightenment and universal love. What may follow is well enough known to any student of history.

JOHN STUART MILL, THE BNP, AND THE UK'S DYING DEMOCRACY (2011)[105]

For about a year now, I have been writing for *VDare* about the British National Party (BNP), which is the main white nationalist organisation in the United Kingdom. The essence of my reports has been that the BNP faces a wall of media bias and legal and administrative persecution that put its survival in doubt. Though, as a libertarian, I have my own agenda for England, I do not regard this bias and persecution with any pleasure. What is being done to the BNP is unfair in itself and sets a precedent for the persecution of other dissident organisations and movements. What I have now to report about the BNP must be depressing both to white nationalists and to believers in liberal democracy.

Electoral Embarrassment

First, there is the result of a parliamentary by-election on Thursday the 13th January 2011. The Labour Party won the Oldham and Saddleworth constituency in the 2010 general election. However, the winner was unseated by a legal challenge, and a fresh election was held. The result was very poor for the BNP. It got its lowest ever vote in the constituency. It should, in the nature of things, have done better than to get 1,560 votes and take fifth place. There is no reason why the party should have won this election. The British electoral system has always been biased against small parties, and a BNP victory would have required something like a miracle. But it should have done better. A by-election has none of the pressure of a general election—no one goes off to vote thinking that his vote *might* decide the next government: people are more inclined to vote for small parties.

Add to this that none of the main parties was looking very attractive. The Labour Party is out of government, and has a leader generally seen as useless. The Liberal Democrats, who came second at the general election, are members of a coalition government that has failed to

---

[105] First published on *www.vdare*.com on the 19th January 2011. My thanks to Peter Brimelow for his permission to republish it here.

The UK's Dying Democracy

generate enthusiasm among the public. The Conservatives ran a minimal campaign and effectively invited people to vote Liberal Democrat.

Moreover, the BNP had been claiming for years that Moslem gangs were targeting young white girls for sexual abuse and forced prostitution. This had been ignored by the mainstream media. Then, a few days before the vote, two Asian men were sent to prison for sexually abusing white girls and forcing them into prostitution. A former Labour Home Secretary then admitted[106] that this was a wider problem than people liked to admit.

All this, and the BNP still did badly. Why it did badly can be explained by any number of reasons. We might say that the British people have looked hard at the BNP and not liked it. Or we might say that the media bias against the BNP was so extreme, that 1,560 votes were a good showing. Or we might look at disunity within the local party. Or we might look at any number of other more or less credible reasons. My own suspicion, for what it is worth, is that the BNP did badly in this by-election because of a general feeling that it is not and will not be successful. This may sound an unusual reason, but, in my experience as a Conservative activist in the 1980s, it is—particular excitements aside—one of the main reasons why people vote for a party or not.

And the BNP was not regarded as successful for reasons that many outside England might regard as perverse. This brings me to my second piece of news. On Friday the 17th December 2010, the BNP finally beat off the case brought against it by the Equality and Human Rights Commission (EHRC). This meant that the assets of the Party would not now be seized, and its leader, Nick Griffin, would not now be sent to prison. It brought to an end around eighteen months of legal harassment by an organisation that has about as much to do with equality and human rights as the Democratic People's Republic of Korea has with democracy or the people or republicanism—but that does have unlimited amounts of the taxpayers' money to throw at whoever or whatever may be disliked by the British ruling class.

I have been covering this case for VDare almost since it began. However, not everyone will have read or will remember my earlier articles. I think, therefore, it would be helpful if I were to summarise its course.

---

[106] *www.bbc.co.uk/news/uk-england-derbyshire-12141603*

The Legal Harassment of the BNP

The EHRC was set up by virtue of the Equality Act 2006. Its alleged function was to bring enforcement of all the "equality" and "human rights" legislation of the past few decades within a central and unified scheme. But it first came to media prominence in August 2009, when it began legal proceedings against the BNP. Its cause of action was that the BNP restricted membership to white people—that is, to "indigenous British ethnic groups deriving from the class of 'Indigenous Caucasian'" plus "those we regard as closely related and ethnically assimilated or assimilable aboriginal members of the European race also resident in Britain."[107] (Which is interpreted to include Jews—thus one BNP elected official, Pat Richardson, a local councilor, is Jewish).

This restriction and others like it had so far been accepted as natural by both members and opponents of the BNP. The party exists, after all, to assert that the British Isles are the homeland of the English, Scottish, Welsh and Irish peoples; and it denies the wisdom and the legitimacy of the mostly state-sponsored immigration of non-whites since the end of the Second World War. Its membership rule was no more controversial than the limitation of places at a Jewish school to Jewish children or the exclusion of practising Moslems from ordination by the Roman Catholic Church. But the lawyers of the EHRC had found that the BNP membership rule might be in breach of sections 24 and 25(5) of the Equality Act and of the Race Relations Act 1976 (as amended). And so began lavishing the taxpayers' money on an action that was ostensibly about the right of non-whites to join a party that disapproved of their presence in the United Kingdom.

In March 2010, the BNP changed its rules and said it would admit non-whites to membership, and it then admitted an elderly Sikh who was a long-standing British nationalist. However, it also imposed two conditions on new members to prevent flooding attempts—that is, to prevent large numbers of non-whites from joining and then bringing actions of their own against the party, or using its internal rules to destroy the party. First, prospective members should be visited at home, to see if they were suitable for membership. Second, all members should declare support for the "continued creation, fostering, maintenance and existence" of an indigenous British race, and should support action

---

[107] Constitution of The British National Party, Eighth Edition, published November 2004.

towards "stemming and reversing" immigration. The EHRC immediately argued that these conditions amounted to "indirect racial discrimination," and continued its case against the BNP.

The EHRC won this round. On the 12th March 2010, a Judge outlawed the requirement for home visits, saying that this might lead to intimidation—though admitting that there was no evidence it ever had. He also outlawed the requirement to declare support for party principle and policy. He said:

> I hold that the BNP are likely to commit unlawful acts of discrimination within section 1b Race Relations Act 1976 in the terms on which they are prepared to admit persons to membership under the 12th addition of their constitution. [108]

The reason for this, the Judge went on, was that no non-white person could support these policies without compromising his "personal sense of self-worth and dignity as a member of their racial group." And so the BNP changed its membership rules again, now accepting members regardless of whether they agreed with its policies.

However, these conditions for membership were only suspended by the BNP, not removed. And so the EHRC went to court again, this time arguing that the BNP was in contempt for not complying in full with the earlier judgment. The penalties for contempt of court are an unlimited fine or two years imprisonment (imprisonment of the most senior person if the defendant is a corporate body).

The hearing took place in London on the 8th and 9th November 2010. Judgment was then reserved for six weeks. It was finally given on Friday the 17th December 2010, and the Judges ruled that the BNP had no case to answer.

The EHRC was plainly disappointed with the judgment. But, according to John Wadham, one of its main officials:

> Today's judgment makes no difference to the substance of our action against the BNP... The County Court ruled that the BNP's constitution was racially discriminatory. That ruling remains in place and has now, finally, been obeyed by the BNP.

108

www.manchestereveningnews.co.uk/news/s/1200216_new_bnp_membership_rules_judged_to_be_biased

Freedom of Speech in England

He added that he and his colleagues would continue monitoring BNP rules relating to members' right to vote and attend meetings and whether such rights were connected with what members thought about mixed-race relationships and the like. "We will be keeping a watching brief on them to make sure they don't break the law," he added.[109]

The End of the Beginning—Perhaps Not Even That!

So far as the British media were concerned, this was the end of the matter. Once the judgment was reported—and reported rather briefly—it is as if some spell of silence had been cast on the gentlemen of the press. Nick Griffin continues to send out his regular newsletters. His followers continue to agitate. But there has been no editorial comment on the judgement, and no significant reporting on what might have happened next.

This does not mean that the BNP has struck a blow for freedom that will rank with the Trial of the Seven Bishops, or the Treason Trials of 1794. Anyone who thinks that last month's judgment was the end of the matter is naïve. The EHRC will not go away, and there are so many other avenues of attack on the BNP, from media smears, to private legal actions, to disruption by the security services. And the courts are not neutral. Contempt of court hearings do not usually involve complex issues of law. I find it very suspicious that judgment had to be reserved in this matter for six whole weeks. Rather than for pondering the various submissions, it is more likely that the six weeks were used for asking round among the powerful whether the BNP could decently be put out of the way, or if there was no choice but for justice to be done. I really do not think this will be my last article on the persecution of the BNP.

And this is probably the main reason why the BNP did so badly in the Oldham and Saddleworth by-election. Success of this kind in the courts nowadays indicates that a person or movement has been singled out for destruction.

Liberal Values and the BNP

I will say in passing that none of this can be reconciled with any version of liberalism as it might have been recognised before the name was taken over by American big state managerialists. The only human rights claimed by liberalism are to life, liberty and justly-acquired property. From these follow the specific rights to freedom of speech and freedom

---

[109] BBC Report, 17th December 2010.

of association. This first is the right to say anything about public affairs—no matter how upsetting it may be to others. The second is the right of adults to associate or not as they see fit. No one has the right to be loved. No one has the right to be included. No one has the right not to be hated or ridiculed or despised. We may all have a general obligation to behave decently to others—and it is this on which political correctness is a parasitic growth—but the obligation itself is not one that may rightly be imposed by law.

I could elaborate on the above for several pages. However, I imagine my readers are more interested in the BNP than in libertarian homilies. I have explained that the BNP is marked out for destruction, and that this mark has for the moment depressed its fortunes. Let me then move to a discussion of *why* a small political party like the BNP is under such heavy and continual attack. If it were the sort of organisation it is claimed to be, it would probably be left alone. A party of skinheads and Hitler-worshippers is a wonderful excuse for people who think themselves "progressive" to sit round the dinner table, competitively boasting how many black and homosexual friends they have, and assuring each other of benefits that "diversity" has brought to England.

The truth, I think, is that the BNP is not a national socialist, but a nationalist party. Whatever it may once have been, it is no longer, or is rapidly ceasing to be. And it is the nationalism that makes it so dangerous. Certain nationalisms can be tolerated, and even celebrated—Scotch nationalism, for example, with its sporrans and whines about Culloden, and its ruthless grasping at English subsidies—not to mention its liking for the European Union. But the big fear is that the BNP has already vacated the dead end of national socialism for white nationalism and an equal embrace for all the nationalisms of the British Isles. If it has done this, it might finally see the logic of its position and become an *English* nationalist party. It would then be in a position to speak for an unusually ferocious and cohesive nation. This cannot be risked. If English nationalism were to become an active political force, it would mean the end of the present British ruling class. This would be ended for its general uselessness over much of the past century, and for the legitimising ideology it has, with grim enthusiasm, been trying to impose for at least the past generation.

A Legitimising Ideology Both Anti-Liberal and Anti-National

There is, of course, nothing inherently bad in legitimising ideologies. Every ruling class needs some body of ideas that directly justifies its

Freedom of Speech in England

position, and that also supports those institutions and state of affairs that entrench that position. And, so far as ruling classes are inseparable from states, the only question—this side of a libertarian utopia—is how much respect a ruling class ideology pays to the lives, liberties and property of ordinary people. The problem for England, though, is that the present ruling class has taken up a legitimising ideology that involves the flattening of popular rights. It sees itself less as a committee of trustees for the nation than as the senior management for a "community of communities." Mass-immigration of non-whites has been made a policy of state. Objections to this have been made increasingly illegal. "Diversity" is a blessing, and anyone who fails to agree must be ruthlessly bullied. See, for example, this by Andrew Marr, formerly the Political Editor of BBC News:

> [T]he final answer, frankly, [after miscegenation, school propaganda, and higher taxes to pay for it all] is the vigorous use of state power to coerce and repress. It may be my Presbyterian background, but I firmly believe that repression can be a great, civilising instrument for good. Stamp hard on certain 'natural' beliefs for long enough and you can almost kill them off. The police are first in line to be burdened further, but a new Race Relations Act will impose the will of the state on millions of other lives too.[110]

Now, the primary motivation of this is not to destroy the white race, or to turn Britain into an Islamic state—though there is always more than one agenda at work in a project of this nature. Nor is it the creation of a heavily-policed theme park in which imams and transgendered lesbians and football fans and rap singers all pretend to love each other. In my book, *Cultural Revolution, Culture War: How Conservatives Lost England, and how to Get it Back*, I do argue at some length how Britain—and perhaps America—have been taken over from within by a clique of neo-Marxists, who are trying to impose every multicultural and politically correct fantasy of their student days. This is true. There is no doubt that the intellectual and governing *élites* of both countries are soaked in the thought of Antonio Gramsci and Louis Althusser and Michel Foucault. At the same time, though, I believe that political correctness and multiculturalism are symptoms as well as causes. The gathering attack on representative liberal democracy is more a purpose in itself than a by-product of present intellectual trends.

---

[110] Andrew Marr, "Poor? Stupid? Racist? Then don't listen to a pampered white liberal like me," *The Guardian*, London, 28th February 1999.

The UK's Dying Democracy

One of the main reasons for this is that a reasonably homogeneous nation state may not be democratic, but it *can be* democratic. People who have a common identity will often conceive common interests, and stand together against a government that does not respect these interests. They may also trust each other with political power—confident that differences over economic or other policies will not be carried to the point of civil war.

This is a standard argument of nationalists. But it is also accepted within a significant strand of classical liberalism. A hundred and fifty years ago, John Stuart Mill stated the argument about as clearly as it can be. In Chapter 16 of his essay On Representative Government, he says:

> Free institutions are next to impossible in a country made up of different nationalities. Among a people without fellow-feeling, especially if they read and speak different languages, the united public opinion, necessary to the working of representative government, cannot exist. The influences which form opinions and decide political acts are different in the different sections of the country. An altogether different set of leaders have the confidence of one part of the country and of another. The same books, newspapers, pamphlets, speeches, do not reach them. One section does not know what opinions, or what instigations, are circulating in another. The same incidents, the same acts, the same system of government, affect them in different ways; and each fears more injury to itself from the other nationalities than from the common arbiter, the state. Their mutual antipathies are generally much stronger than jealousy of the government. That any one of them feels aggrieved by the policy of the common ruler is sufficient to determine another to support that policy. Even if all are aggrieved, none feel that they can rely on the others for fidelity in a joint resistance; the strength of none is sufficient to resist alone, and each may reasonably think that it consults its own advantage most by bidding for the favour of the government against the rest. [111]

One of the reasons why England was, in the nineteenth and most of the twentieth centuries the model of representative liberal democracies was that it was remarkably homogeneous. Ireland was always an exception—but it was another island, and could for most of the time be ignored. But the Scottish and Welsh nations were broadly willing to fit themselves into an English structure. This meant that there were none of those national or regional diversities that made representative government difficult or impossible in much of Europe.

---

[111] *philosophy.eserver.org/mill-representative-govt.txt*

To be sure, England never became a pure democracy. The people at large were allowed to give final answers to questions—but the questions themselves were always put by a largely aristocratic ruling class. But this ruling class retained power on the understanding that it would identify itself with the interests of the whole nation.

The old ruling class was destroyed by two great wars. It was destroyed in the sense that disproportionate numbers of its own young were killed in the fighting, and by the high taxes and the socialist challenge that attended these wars. And it allowed itself to be destroyed so far as it had identified with the nation. There was no shirking from military service, and few attempts to conceal taxable wealth. Moreover, these were *democratic* wars. The first one, in particular, had to be sold at its outset to what might otherwise have been a sceptical public. The necessary lies then generated national hatreds so intense that the war itself ran out of control.

Globalisation + Mass-Immigration = Unaccountable Class Domination

The managerialist ruling class that emerged after 1945 has been resolutely anti-nationalist and anti-democratic. It has signed the county up to every treaty in sight that would transfer power to unaccountable, and frequently invisible, transnational bodies in which it could have a leading place. Most obviously, it lied the country into the European Union. This was a creation of European ruling classes that had faced similar problems of national over-identification; and its central purpose has been to concentrate real power into a cartel of ruling classes, thereby allowing these to float away from accountability. Few members of the new ruling class in England have military inclinations—though they are happy enough to sacrifice other people's sons when it suits their convenience. They derive much of their wealth from involvement in multinational business, or in multinational bureaucracies, or in the implementation of treaty commitments; and they cannot be touched financially short of a revolution.

Mass-immigration has been the domestic counterpart of globalisation. The second transfers power upwards. The first so Balkanises national politics and social life that no concerted effort can be made to pull power down again to the people. We are moving quickly to the situation described by Mill—where "the strength of none is sufficient to resist alone, and each may reasonably think that it consults its own advantage most by bidding for the favour of the government against the rest." I think what he had in mind was the Hapsburg Empire, where Slavs had recently been used to put down German and Hungarian revolts, and where German and Hungarian nationalism was then encouraged to keep the Slavs in line. That, minus the high culture, is what the British ruling class has in mind for England. It wants a country in which political argument is either to be suppressed on the grounds of good communal relations, or is worthless because all elections are fought on communal lines, and their results always mirror the census returns.

I am not claiming that there is an overt conspiracy. I have discussed the above analysis with many journalists and politicians. All have denied it. Many have been incredulous. I do not think they were lying to me. This may indicate that I am wrong. Just as easily, it indicates that, while there are individual conspiracies—getting us into and keeping us in the European Union, for example, or getting us into the Iraq and Afghan Wars—there is no single overarching conspiracy of dispossession. But there does not need to be any such conspiracy. Political correctness and multiculturalism did not become parts of a legitimising ideology because thousands of well-connected students just happened to be lectured after 1968 into believing them. Nor was it because the well-connected thought they might be useful as domestic counterparts to globalisation. Without any visible coordination, groups of people often act as if directed. Everything I have mentioned can be explained in terms of ideas, and the material interests conceived in terms of these ideas, and the personalities of those involved.

Equally, the almost fanatical hatred directed against the BNP is not consciously the product of the fear that English nationalism might bring about a revolution. However at variance with the truth they may be, the reasons given for hatred are mostly believed by those giving them. But, I repeat, it is not distaste for what it is said to be that really drives persecution of the BNP. It is fear of what the BNP might become, and of the great reaction it might contribute to enabling.

I will not say that the BNP will be destroyed. Its electoral fortunes may recover. England is not a fully totalitarian country, and there are limits to what even a frightened ruling class can do. But, purely so far as it might become successful, the BNP is certainly marked for destruction. I do not think this will be my last article on the matter.

DEFENDING THE RIGHT TO DENY THE HOLOCAUST—ONE (1996)[112]

I ordered this report expecting it to be another long moan about the Internet—how it enables holocaust revisionists and anti-semites to have their say, free from the usual means of shutting them up. In the event, I was pleasantly surprised. The report is a very good summary of the debate over free speech on the Internet. It is clear, informative, and—on the whole—balanced. It acknowledges that free speech is important. See, for example:

> Arguably, the freedom of speech provided by the Internet and its resistance to controls, especially by governments, should not be lightly abandoned. Throughout history, those in authority have sought to restrict, if not suppress altogether, the expression of independent, critical, and unfashionable ideas and beliefs. [p.13]

Of course, I agree with this, and commend whoever wrote it for writing it so well. The problem with the report is not that its authors are lying bigots, but that they have made a fault of judgement. The above quotation continues:

> However, as has often been pointed out, the Internet epitomizes the classic 'liberal dilemma'. In this case maintaining the principle of free speech means extending that right to those who would use it to 'promote violence, threaten women, denigrate minorities, promote homophobia and conspire against democracy'. [*ibid*]

Here I disagree. There is no such dilemma. There is a case for punishing someone who incites offences against life or property at a time when he knows that his listeners are already out of their right minds. He is then using those people as an instrument of his will, rather as if he were pulling the strings of a puppet. But my understanding of liberalism is that all other forms of speech are to be absolutely unhindered. Indeed, note my use of "rather" in the previous sentence. I can think of very few cases—

---

[112] Review of *The Governance of Cyberspace: The Far Right on the Internet*, by David Capitanchik and Michael Whine, Institute for Jewish Policy Research, London, 1996, 16pp. Published in *Free Life*, 26, December 1996.

governments and criminal conspiracies are another matter—where someone acts so completely under the will of another that this other ought to be held responsible for whatever crimes result. Punish those who push lighted rags through a letter box, but leave alone those whose writings condone or even incite such acts.

I know that for many Jews this sounds a bizarre statement. If I had been lectured all my childhood about pogroms and gas chambers, I might feel nervous about some of the literature now available on the Internet. But, though understandable, this is to be resisted. In the first place, there is no international Nazi conspiracy—certainly nothing that needs the kind of attention called for. Most active anti-semites are pitiable cranks, like Colin Jordan or Lady Birdwood. Many others are in the movement for the gay sex or as police spies. The sort of stuff one reads about in *Searchlight* or in Anti-Defamation League reports is very largely fantasy. Why this stuff is put out, and why so many people claim to believe it, are matters beyond my present scope. But the reason is not always honest mistake based on fears of renewed persecution.

In the second place, most "hate" literature on the Internet is not incitement to illegal acts, but claims about matters of fact—usually about whether the received account of the holocaust is the true one. The reply to these claims should not be calls for censorship, as at present, but open debate. Whatever feelings it may arouse in its victims and their descendants, the holocaust is an historical event like any other. As such, it must be open to any interpretation or view of its reality, no matter how malevolent these may appear. The received account must not be given the same privileged status as the core doctrines of Christianity still—regrettably—enjoy in this country.

And—as is said again and again in this journal—there is no surer way to promote holocaust revision and anti-semitism than to make them illegal. The revisionists are unlikely ever to win an open debate. But their enemies seem determined to lose the shadow debate now taking place. The most obvious effect of censorship would be to raise up a small army of martyrs, their faults obscured by their willingness to suffer. Even to call for censorship is stupid. What are people supposed to think of a truth that is supported less by argument than by threats of prison?

However, the debate covered by this report is about the Internet, not the Jews. Certainly, organisations like the Simon Wiesenthal Center and the Board of Deputies of British Jews have made contemptible fools of themselves in the debate. But it must never be forgotten that there is no

Freedom of Speech in England

such thing as "the Jews." There are Jews on both sides of this debate, and there are Jews on no side at all; and those on our side are among the most relentless and uncompromising advocates of freedom of speech. And even if the Jews on the censorship side were to fall silent, the clamour against the Internet would continue almost as loud as before. If it were not the holocaust, it would be something else. Indeed, in this country, it is something else: it is child pornography. The truth is that what the Internet allows is so powerful, so destructive of so many established interests, that its enemies can hardly be counted.

And what the Internet allows is freedom of speech. Yes, this means freedom for nazis and paedophiles to give endless offence. But, far more importantly, it means freedom for public opinion to be reborn as it used to exist before about 1910. Since then in England, the media has at least distorted the news. Instead of reflecting what people are really thinking, and reporting what the politicians are really doing, it has created a world close enough in appearances to the real one not to cause scandal, but in which nearly all the substance has been replaced. It may no longer be able to conceal things like the Abdication Crisis, or Churchill's drunken incompetence. But it can still set a false agenda for public debate. It does this by a subtle yet effective framing of arguments, by turns of phrase, by terminology. We have, for example, the continued use of "right" and "left"—a dichotomy that never meant much at its most relevant, and which now describes political debate about as well as the Ptolemaic system described the universe. It is a dichotomy that, so far as public is concerned, serves to break libertarianism into disconnected fragments and to scatter these across the whole conventional spectrum of thought, and so to reduce its effectiveness as the main opposition ideology of our age. Or we have the repeated conflation of greenery with niceness, of coercive altruism with caring, of markets with throat-cutting greed, of anti-nationalism with a love of supra-national institutions like the United Nations and the European Union. It seems paranoid to say this in a country where no laws exist against propagating any point of view, but the issues are presented by the British media in ways that often prevent their being intelligently discussed. Part of this, no doubt, is due to the idleness and stupidity of most people who get jobs in the media. Part of it, though, is the effect of a centralised media the owners of which have been co-opted into the Establishment.

The Internet changes all this. The West is moving perceptibly into an age of zero censorship. We are not there yet—not even in America, where the revolution is most advanced. But it is plain where we are heading.

The Right to Deny the Holocaust—One

The intricate web of laws and informal pressures that governs expression in even the freest countries is being broken through. If we want to publish unorthodox opinions, we no longer need to negotiate with editors, hoping at best for a letter to be published or to be laughed at even while allowed on to a current affairs programme. If we want to read such opinions, we no longer need to hunt down obscure little pamphlets and newsletters. It is increasingly irrelevant whether the media barons are offered bribes or threatened with prison: their ability to manipulate what we read or see or hear is withering almost by the day. If still only in small amounts, everything is now available on the Internet, and can be accessed as easily as looking for a Chinese takeaway in the *Yellow Pages*. And every day, more pages are created on the World Wide Web, and more data flows through the newsgroups. We are increasingly in a position to know what is happening, and to make our opinions about this directly available to millions of other people.

No wonder the Internet is hated. No wonder the established media outlets are choked with lurid tales of what corruption lurks on it, just waiting to pounce on children and the weak minded. It must be controlled before it can destroy the great counter-Enlightenment of our century.

Again, I thank the Institute for Jewish Policy Research for having produced so interesting a report. Even so, I do greatly regret that it is on the wrong side in this debate. I should have expected Jews, of all people, to fear censorship of any kind, and to recall what horrors of arbitrary government can flourish without the censure of a truly free press.

DEFENDING THE RIGHT
TO DENY THE HOLOCAUST—TWO (2007)[113]

Last week, on the 19th April [2007], the Justice Ministers of the European Union agreed to make "incitement to racism and xenophobia" a criminal offence in all 27 member states. Despite the best efforts of the German Government, this does not mean that sceptical comments on the holocaust will become a crime in any European country where it is not so already. I am surprised that the British Government held out for a moderating of the final document so that all speech short of "incitement" will remain free. But I doubt if the agreement made last week will be the last word in the matter. Already, nine member states of the European Union punish denial or "gross revision" with imprisonment. There are calls for criminalisation in England. I have no doubt these calls will grow louder.

My own view—and I speak on this matter not only for me but also for the Libertarian Alliance—is that there should be no restrictions on freedom of speech where public affairs are concerned. This involves, among much else, the right to say anything at all about politics, religion, sex, science or history. It is no business of the State to tell people what they can and cannot think. Our bodies are our own. Our minds are our own. What we do with them is our business. It is one of the highest glories of the Enlightenment that states were shamed out of dragooning people into the various established worships of Europe. It is one of the most ominous signs of the modern counter-Enlightenment that people can again be persecuted for their opinions.

Of course, there are people who claim to believe in freedom of speech, but who say that the promotion of "hatred" is a distinct matter. They say that "hate speech" is direct or indirect incitement to acts of violence against others, and so should be put down by law. This is not, on their reasoning, censorship. It is simply a matter of keeping the peace.

---

[113] Published on *www.seangabb.co.uk* on the 24th April 2007.

The Right to Deny the Holocaust—Two

We in the Libertarian Alliance reject this supposed distinction. What some call the promotion of hatred others call telling the truth. Quite often, whatever opinion the rich and powerful do not like they will find some means of calling "hatred." In any event, we believe in the right to promote hatred by any means that do not fall within the Common Law definition of assault.

Perhaps you are one of those people who believe in a distinction between free speech and hate speech. This being so, I will drop any further mention of abstract rights and turn to a practical argument that is ultimately just as connected with keeping the peace. Let me ask: what reason have I to believe that the holocaust really happened?

The obvious answer—that the standard history books say it happened—is not in itself much good. My first degree was in History, and I know enough about certain periods to say with confidence that even standard secondary sources are riddled with errors that sometimes amount to actual falsehoods. I will not discuss the numerous claims of doubtful truth made about the Later Roman Empire. I will only observe that, in the standard accounts of the Second World War, the Katyn Wood massacre used to be blamed on the Germans, and now it is blamed on the Soviets. How can I be sure that the same is not true for the holocaust?

The next answer—that there are many witnesses to the holocaust still alive—is also not much good in itself. These people may have been in a concentration camp, and they may have seen atrocities. They did not see the holocaust in any synoptic sense. They may have been mistaken. One of my grandmothers, for example, lived in Kent all through the Second World War, and she went to her grave insisting that there had been an unsuccessful German invasion of England in 1940. There are millions of people who claim to have seen plaster statues of the Virgin weep real tears, and I am perfectly assured they are mistaken or lying. How do I not know that the holocaust survivors I have met or seen on television were not mistaken or lying?

Or there is the argument from the agreed nature of the Hitler *Régime*. Almost everyone accepts that this acted in defiance of—and perhaps in open contempt for—the norms of civilised behaviour. This may be evidence for the probability of a holocaust. But it is hardly proof that one happened. On the same reasoning, I can believe that Hitler was a bad man: this does not require me to believe that he ate human flesh.

To answer the question properly for myself, of whether the holocaust happened, I need skills and knowledge that I do not have and do not feel inclined to acquire. I need a good understanding of German, Polish, Russian, Hungarian and Hebrew, among other languages. I need to be able to track down a mass of primary sources, most of which are unpublished but are in various European and American archives. To evaluate all this, I need technical knowledge that I do not have—knowledge, for instance, about the lethal nature of Zyklon B gas, or of diesel fumes, or of how to burn bodies and dispose of the remains.

I have not read even much of the secondary material that exists in English. This is not a subject that has interested me since I sat my O Levels. I have, though, read a very small selection of the material published on both sides of the debate. And what I can say of this is that, considered purely in itself, the revisionist material is as persuasive as that of the mainstream historians. At least one side in this debate is lying, and lying very fluently—but I am not able, on the basis of the evidence offered, to say who is lying.

Nevertheless, I believe with reasonable firmness that the German National Socialists did try, during the last years of the Second World War, to murder every Jew they could set hands on, and that they succeeded in murdering several million. Whether this was a plan centrally conceived and centrally directed, or whether most of the killings were deliberate murder or the effects of culpable negligence, are not matters on which I have any opinion. But on the central claim of the holocaust, I am reasonably assured.

I am assured of this on the authority of the mainstream historians. I have no means of knowing for myself whether the holocaust happened. But I take it on trust that it did happen. That is true for me, and it is true for the overwhelming majority of everyone else who believes the same.

There is nothing in its nature unsatisfactory about knowledge based on authority. Most of what we know we cannot demonstrate on any grounds of direct evidence. I "know," for example, that light travels at 186,000 miles per second, and that the Earth is in an elliptical orbit around the Sun, and that the Earth is around 5,000 million years old. I am completely incapable of demonstrating any of this. I might even have trouble arguing with a convinced flat-earther. I believe all these things and much more beside because nearly everyone else believes them.

I grant that we should not believe too much on authority when we are competent to investigate it for ourselves. But the only real concern with such knowledge is not that it is on authority, but that the authority should be good. What makes authority good? The best answer is when it can be

The Right to Deny the Holocaust—Two

openly contested by others who claim to know better, but who have not convinced reasonable onlookers that they do.

With regard to the holocaust, I have—broadly speaking—two options. I can believe that it did happen roughly as claimed. Or I can believe that it is a gigantic conspiracy of lies maintained since the 1940s in the face of all evidence. Since debate remains free in the English-speaking world, it should be obvious what I am to believe. I believe in the central fact of the holocaust. On the secondary issues mentioned above, where my authorities do not agree, I suspend judgment.

Take away the freedom to argue with or against these authorities, though, and my assurance that they are right must be weakened.

In my case, let me say, laws against revising or denying the holocaust will not destroy my belief that it happened. There is still the long preceding time of open debate, and the unlikelihood that compelling new evidence either way has been discovered now. There is also the fact that many people will insist on laws in support of evident truths. If you are Jewish, for example, it may be very upsetting for people to say that your grandparents were not murdered in Poland in 1944, but are alive and well and living in Finchley. Or you may worry that scepticism about the holocaust will prepare the way for a repeat of it. Then there are the obvious financial and moral advantages that certain Jews and the State of Israel have obtained from the holocaust. Cries of anti-semitism are a good closing tactic for many debates that might otherwise be lost.

Laws to compel belief in the holocaust do not mean it did not happen. But they do allow people to ask what kind of truth this is that needs laws to defend it. There are many people who know even less about the holocaust than I do, and who deny that it happened simply because David Irving is generally acknowledged to be an expert of sorts on the period, and he had to be locked up before he would shut up.

Open mockery of deeply-held views, deliberate and gross offence, savage abuse that barely stops short of incitement to violence—these may well disturb the peace. Far worse, though, is the sort of hatred that boils beneath a seemingly placid surface, and then erupts into a disorder that cannot be checked by reason. That is the danger of laws to compel belief in the holocaust.

And they make cranks into martyrs. Do you suppose the Libertarian Alliance enjoys putting out news releases in defence of David Irving? We put these out because we believe in freedom of speech with no exceptions. We put up with the cold shoulder from other civil liberties groups, and with raised eyebrows and outright smears. We are much happier defending the rights of sexual or social minorities, whose tastes we might ourselves share or do not think in the least reprehensible. We do what we believe is our duty, and do it as well as we can—but we regret the need to do it.

And they set a precedent for further censorship. If people must be careful what they say about the holocaust, why not add the alleged Armenian genocide? Or the alleged Bosnian genocide? Or the alleged Irish genocide of the 1840s? Or the Divine Mission of Christ? Or the holiness of the Prophet? Why not have legal curbs on doubts regarding the nature and extent of global warming? Indeed, on this last, there are calls for the American President to be impeached for his expressed doubts.

Censorship is rather like torture. It is always possible to fabricate "exceptional circumstances" to justify it. Opponents can always be denounced as naive or tender-hearted. But it is always corrupting of civilised decency. Its general tendency is to undermine whatever it is called into being to uphold.

I am glad that the British Government, among others, managed on this occasion to prevent a common scheme of censorship across the European Union. But I do not suppose, given the settled decline of faith in freedom of speech, that this will turn out to have been more than a holding action.

REVIEW OF A PRESS LICENSING BILL (1993)[114]

This is a "book of evidence" compiled from written and oral submissions to a Special Parliamentary Committee, assembled to consider the Freedom and Responsibility of the Press Bill tabled by Clive Soley MP.

It is in every respect an extraordinary work. It is the first private publication of the transcript of a Parliamentary Committee and of all the evidence placed before it. It also records the first occasion on which Members of Parliament have decided to investigate the issues behind a Bill before it is debated clause by clause at its second reading.

Both these facts are to be welcomed. A private report of Parliamentary proceedings is a step in the right direction. I regret the lack of an ISBN classification: this makes the work unnecessarily hard to find. I also regret the rather amateurish printing error—"sorts" in place of "torts"—to be found in the Libertarian Alliance submission printed on page 138. But these are minor defects, and do not ruin the overall effect.

The procedural device by which the evidence reached the Parliamentary record is an excellent one. The Chairman of the Committee, Patrick Cormack MP, writes in his Preface that

> [f]or some years now there has been provision for this sort of exercise to be undertaken by a standing committee before it considers a Bill clause by clause. It could surely only benefit the quality of our legislation if the process became not an option but an obligation.[p.iii]

The quality of legislation would indeed benefit greatly—though not, I suspect, because Bills would be framed with any higher regard for the public interest, but simply because more consideration for each Bill inevitably will mean fewer Bills.

The Bill itself is another matter. Any Bill which contains the words "Freedom of the Press" is to be suspected. Any Bill which contains the

---

[114] Review of *Report of Special Parliamentary Hearings on Freedom and Responsibility of the Press,* by Mike Jempson (ed), Crantock Communications, Bristol, 1993, 181pp. First published in Free *Life* 18, May 1993.

Freedom of Speech in England

words "Freedom and Responsibility of the Press" may safely be denounced unread as a censor's charter.

However, I have read the Bill, and am able to supply particulars of the censorship to be imposed. Take clause 1:

> There shall be a body, to be called the Independent Press Authority (the Authority), which shall -
>
> (a) seek the presentation of news by newspapers and periodicals with due accuracy;
>
> (b) secure the free dissemination of news and information in the public interest and the promotion of professional and ethical standards;

In pursuit of these ends, the Authority is to exercise a general power of inspection, where not of control. It is to indicate who may and may not own newspapers, and who may and may not write for them. It is to indicate which of them shall and shall not be carried by W.H. Smith and the other big distributors. It is to investigate complaints against individual publications, and its adjudications are to be enforced on application to the High Court of Justice. In short, except all powers but the last are advisory, and there is no requirement to post bonds or submit copy for approval before publication, the Bill is as entire a scheme of censorship as can be imagined.

What, after all, is a duly accurate presentation of news? It is something performed by most of our daily newspapers every day—and it has been performed in this country every day for most of the 298 years since the ending of the last State censorship. It is not perfectly performed, I allow. Indeed, there are newspapers that make money from printing lies; and this is to be deplored. But we live in an imperfect world. The best we can ever hope of our institutions is they will permit good a higher chance of prevailing than evil. This is the case, I assert, with the present market in newspapers, as constrained by the general law of the land. It would not be the case were we to shackle the press with an extensive system of State control. Such systems have been set up in many other countries. In every instance, they have transformed the press from a guardian of freedom into an instrument of despotism.

The advocates of this Bill have repeatedly claimed that its effect will not be to shackle the press, but will simply compel editors to correct factual errors by granting a right of reply. This is true—but not entirely accurate in a general sense. Most of the powers granted to the Authority under the present Bill are, as said, advisory. But advisory powers have a habit in this country of turning compulsive. The press will be urged to comply with the authority's decrees regardless of whether they have any formal force of law. Persistent breaches will be answered with more talk of "drinking at the Last Chance Saloon" and threats of legislation. We have only to look at the history of the "voluntary" agreements with the tobacco industry to see this tendency. Bearing this in mind, we can take the advisory role of the Authority as in fact a power of supervision supported by effective sanctions.

Bearing this in mind, let us examine clause 2-(1) (d) and (e). By these, it shall be the Authority's duty

> to produce and promote codes of professional and ethical standards for the press; [and]

> in support of the duties above, to conduct research into and make recommendations on the training and education of journalists.

This aims very plainly at the licensing of journalists, just as doctors and lawyers are now licensed. No doubt, many journalists will be pleased by licensing. It will limit competition and thereby raise their salaries. It will also create an outermost void into which they can be cast for serious breach of the professional standards imposed on them by the modish bureaucrats who usually get themselves elected or appointed to regulatory bodies.

Forty years ago, licensing would have gone far to preventing the honest discussion of homosexuality which led to the Wolfenden Report and finally to the 1967 Act. Either such discussion would have been too outrageous in itself to be tolerated in a professional body, or it would have provoked the more subtle responses by which such bodies suppress dissent from established values. Today, it would constrain many journalists from denouncing what they find absurd in the gay rights movement. It would expel or simply refuse to license the sort of people who write for *Bulldog* and other national socialist publications—not mention in fundamentalist Islamic, in Moonie, in Trotskyite, or even in libertarian publications.

Other clauses in the Bill, such as those dealing with restrictions on reporting and ownership of newspapers, can easily be turned in the same direction. Perhaps the supporters of the Bill think all this to be a good idea. Perhaps it is. But it cannot, without a gross perversion of language, be described as extending or even preserving the freedom of the press.

Freedom of Speech in England

As I write, the future of this particular Bill is in some doubt. But I have no doubt that something very like it will eventually become law. Perhaps then we shall hear no more complaints of press misconduct, for it will then be perfect in the opinion of those who matter.

STATE REGULATION OF THE BRITISH PRESS: SO WHAT? (2012)[115]

At the moment in England, our masters and their clients are discussing censorship of the newspaper press. After months of submissions, a government inquiry into newspaper conduct has finished, and its report will almost certainly call for what is called "a rule-based framework of regulation." The surface argument is between those who want controls backed by the law, and those who want "voluntary self-regulation." No one who matters, though, disputes that something must be done.

This means that something will be done. And this something will be formal censorship. Even if we start out with one of the minimal options, the desired end is plain. This is for newspapers to be brought under the same formal control as the broadcast media. They will be licensed. They will be subject to various forms of prior restraint. There will be review and complaints procedures for articles already published. The whole process will be managed by the usual ruling class apparatchiks, all on vast salaries, and all enforcing conformity to the usual totalitarian PC.

Now, I know that my duty as a libertarian is to start jumping up and down in defence of our free press. And I will go through the motions. We already have too many controls in this country on what can be published. These are generally used to keep wrongdoing by the rich and powerful from the public eye—that, or to keep us from knowing the truth about the caring, sharing, multi-cultural paradise that is modern England. The effect of more control will be to block future exposure of fraud and bribe-taking by Members of Parliament. Oh—and there is the matter of those ruling class salaries and pensions. I don't know about you, but the great army in modern England of looters in suits—with their low-grade intellects and first-class connections, and their £400,000 salaries at my expense, and their endless public moralising about how everyone else should be made to live—they really get on my tits. Anything that means

---

[115] First published in *The Libertarian Enterprise,* November 2012. My thanks to L. Neil Smith for permission to republish it here.

Freedom of Speech in England

more for these, or more of these, gets my thumb straight in the down position.

This being said, how much difference will actual censorship make to the quality of investigation and news reporting in the newspapers? In a sense, the question answers itself. If it were likely to make no difference, why bother discussing it? If true, however, this answer is of limited value. I admit that, in the past few years, the newspapers have brought down scumbag after scumbag. The most recent example is Denis Macshane, a Labour MP and former Minister who was shown to have milked his expenses by about as much as many of his electors earn in a lifetime of toil. Then there was David Laws, forced to resign as a Minister when it came out that he was getting the taxpayers to underwrite his relationship with his boyfriend—I notice, by the way, he's a Minister again. Or there was Liam Fox, also forced out of office when we learned about the very fishy dealings of his close friend.

Never mind whether *The Sun* newspaper hacked the mobile telephones of various entertainment celebrities—it strikes me as obvious that the purpose of "regulation" will be to stop future embarrassments like the cases given above.

And that's about the limit of the value we get from the newspapers. I suppose they're worth defending for that limited value. But it's hardly worth rolling out long quotes from John Milton and John Stuart Mill. The cases given above are exceptions to the general rule, which is for the newspapers to collaborate in hiding—or simply never to notice—wrongdoing in high places. Look at these cases:

1. In 2007, the BBC announced that, following a meeting with 28 "top environmental scientists" the year before, it would no longer pretend to give balanced coverage of the debate on man-made climate change. Instead, it would become a naked propagandist for the global warming scam. No salaried newspaper reporter bothered to ask who these 28 experts were, and what were their scientific credentials. It took five years before an independent blogger, Tony Newbery, got round to putting in a Freedom of Information request for the names of these experts. When the BBC sent a team of lawyers into action to get a biased tribunal to slap this request down, it was another blogger, Maurizio Morabito (*Omnologos*), who dug round the Web until he found the full list, and showed that these 28 experts were mostly the usual riders on the global warming bandwagon. It became plain that the BBC, which is "public

service broadcaster" with a legal duty of impartiality, was up to its neck in a gigantic intellectual fraud.

After the event, Melanie Phillips wrote a nice article about all this in *The Daily Mail*. It would have been a nicer article, of course, if she and her friends had lifted so much as a finger of their own to expose the fraud.

2. Cyril Smith was a Liberal Party politician, and supposedly the fattest Member of Parliament in history. He was also a pederast with a taste for beating young boys. In 1991, I had dinner with a retired Special Branch officer. He told me how, in 1977, the Rochdale police had assembled a dossier of evidence against the MP—systematic abuse of homeless boys in a hostel he'd helped found. However, the man was Chief Liberal Whip at the time, and the Liberals were in an informal coalition with a minority Labour Government. My friend was given the job of driving up to Rochdale to confiscate the dossier, and tell the local police to mind their own business in future.

I thought this was very amusing, but only half believed it. The Internet was still in the future, and, however crass their actions, I still took it for granted that England was ruled by men of reasonably spotless integrity. Well, Cyril Smith died in 2010, and it came out that he really had been beating and—so far as his shape allowed—buggering every boy who fell into his clutches.

Not a peep, while he lived, in the mainstream media, of course. So much for the Fourth Estate of the Realm!

3. I suppose I should mention the Jimmy Savile scandal. But this has been done to death, and you need to be very American indeed not to have heard something about it. Again, though, it was pretty common knowledge that he was partial to underage girls. I heard about it when I was a schoolboy. He always looked like a dirty old man. Despite this, when he died in 2011, the newspaper press went into a chorus of his praises. It took a whole year for him to be demoted to his current—though temporary—status of most prolific sex offender in history.

More important, though, than the details of what Jimmy Savile might or might not have done in a caravan in Skegness c.1973 is what the sudden eruption of the scandal wiped from all the newspapers. Fringe organisations like the British National Party had long been pointing to a culture of sexual predation among Pakistani Moslems in the North of England. There were whole gangs of these people involved in the kidnap and rape of white working class girls. The police had ignored every complaint. Ditto local authorities. Anyone who complained too loudly was called a racist and threatened with formal or informal punishments. Finally, the scale of criminality reached a point where the authorities were forced to act. A series of trials in the first half of 2012 provided chapter and verse evidence about the real nature of race relations in England. This had to be reported by the newspapers and commented on by its appointed writers. They even had to report police claims that one murdered white girl had been disposed of in a mincing machine and sold as doner kebabs.

Very convenient, don't you think, that the stuttering discussion of race and immigration all this forced the authorities into allowing was immediately smothered by full spectrum coverage of the alleged crimes of the late Jimmy Savile?

I could go on. I believe that the transfer of Hong Kong was set in motion, back in 1982, by a few London banks that wanted privileged access to the China market. I could give you the names of the Cabinet Ministers who were bribed into beginning a transfer that no one in Peking had asked for. But they are still alive and very rich, so I won't. I believe that William Hague was either bribed or blackmailed by the Americans into losing the 2001 general election to Labour—Tony Blair having been regarded as more reliably pro-American. I believe many other things. Just because I have no evidence for them doesn't make them untrue. Just because some of them sound outlandish doesn't make me mad. Bearing in mind what we know the newspapers haven't reported, or have conspired to cover up, all of the above and much more beside is conceivably true.

And I'm not the only man in England to have noticed the utter worthlessness of the newspapers. Look at these daily sales figures for the national press:

Title[116]	2012	2000
The Sun	2,582,301	3,557,336
Daily Mail	1,945,496	2,353,915
Daily Mirror	1,102,810	2,270,543

[116] Source: Adapted from *Wikipedia*

Title[116]	2012	2000
Daily Telegraph	578,774	1,039,749
Daily Express	577,543	1,050,846
The Times	397,549	726,349
Financial Times	316,493	435,478
Daily Record	291,825	626,646
The Guardian	215,988	401,560
The Independent	105,160	222,106

Yes, censorship is always bad, and that's what the ruling class is talking about. But why go through more than the motions in defence of a newspaper press as worthless and generally corrupt as the one we have? And, of course, censored or otherwise, there soon won't be much of a newspaper press in England to defend or attack.

To the Reader

Many thanks for buying this book. Many thanks for reading it. Sales of my books are useful to my finances, and they help assure me that I have not been typing away without hope of influence and fame. If you liked it, please consider leaving a review on your local Amazon. Reviews are very important for further sales. Even if you disagree with what I have said, please go ahead and review the book.

You may also wish to look up some of my other books on Amazon. There are many of these. Under my own name, Sean Gabb, I write both non-fiction and fiction. Under the pen-name, Richard Blake, I am writing a long series of historical novels set in the early Byzantine Empire. There are now twelve of these, and they have been commercially translated into half a dozen languages. Though not overtly political, they do manage to reflect my general view of life, and may be of interest. I might add that, in hard copy, they make interesting presents for those hard-to-please loved ones!

Otherwise, please feel free to connect with me on Facebook and on various other social media platforms. Or feel free to contact me directly—*sean@seangabb.co.uk*, or *via* my websites:

https://www.seangabb.co.uk/
http://www.richardblake.me.uk/
http://www.classicstuition.co.uk/

Best regards,

Sean Gabb
Deal

INDEX

A

Abdication 122
Afro-Caribbean 71
Albigenses 9
Alibhai-Brown, Yasmin 42, 49, 52, 53
Althusser, Louis 79, 116
American Renaissance 67, 68, 69, 86, 87
Anglican 7, 12
Annan Report 13
Anti-Defamation League 121
Arts Council England 90
Astor Theatre 77, 80, 81, 82
Avengers 30
Avila, St Theresa of 27
Aztec 84

B

Bacon, Francis 25
Ballet 90
Baudelaire, Charles 8
BBC ..... ix, 11, 20, 21, 37, 41, 42, 43, 44, 46, 52, 54, 60, 67, 72, 114, 116, 134
BBFC 11, 25, 26, 27, 28, 32
Bible 9, 13, 51, 64
Birdwood, Lady 121
Black Police Association 44, 97
Blair, Tony 32, 52, 87, 93, 99, 136
BNP 41, 42, 43, 51, 68, 69, 77, 79, 80, 83, 84, 85, 86, 87, 88, 89, 90, 91, 92, 93, 94, 95, 96, 97, 98, 99, 104, 105, 106, 107, 108, 109, 110, 111, 112, 113, 114, 115, 119
Board of Deputies of British Jews 121
Bombings 60
Brady, Ian .... vii, 8
Brand, Jo .... vi, 41, 42, 43, 46, 47
Brave New World viii
Britain 2, 4, 6, 11, 12, 14, 30, 77, 91, 95, 100, 102, 105, 112, 116
Broadcasting 20, 21, 61
Brown, Gordon 42, 47, 49, 52, 87

Bulldog 131
Bundy, Ted 7
Bunglawala, Inayat 91, 92
Burroughs, William S. 2

C

Callaghan, James 13
Cameron, David 42, 52, 72
Cannibalism 23
Carpenter. Edward 88
Catholic Church 25, 69, 101, 112
Catullus, Gaius Valerius 4, 5
Censorship 8, 1, 11, 13, 128
Chamberlain, Emma 11, 77, 80, 81, 82
Chatterley, Lady 2, 10, 12
Chikatilo, Andrei 10
Children .... ix, xi, xii, 34
Christ 9, 27, 69, 128
Christianity .... viii, 5, 9, 27, 63, 121
Churchill, Winston 122
Clarkson, Jeremy 41, 43, 44, 47, 72
Cobain, Ian 90, 91, 93
Commission for Racial Equality 43
Communist 9, 63, 99
Compton, Gareth 49, 50
Conegate Case 17, 18
Conservative Party ... 1, 2, 29, 49, 65, 88, 94
Copeland, David 68
Copernicus, Nicolas 25
Corbyn, Jeremy 87
Corcoran, Clodagh 23
Coroners and Justice Act 2009 .... ix, xiv
Council of Europe xiv
Counter-Reformation 9
Covington, Harold 108
Criminal Justice Act 1988 35
Critias 2
Crown Prosecution Service xvi
Cumberbatch Report 7
Currie, Edwina 60, 64

D

Daily Express 37, 137
Daily Mail ... 32, 37, 42, 43, 53, 135, 136
Daily Mirror 136
Daily Telegraph 8, 10, 17, 18, 24, 37, 41, 42, 98, 137
Darwinism vi
de Sade, Marquis .... vii, 8, 9
Dio Cassius 8
Diversity 116
Don Giovanni 92
Drugs xi
Dumas, Alexandre 11

E

England. 3, 4, x, xi, xvi, xx, 5, 13, 14, 25, 31, 32, 41, 42, 44, 45, 47, 50, 51, 53, 60, 66, 67, 70, 71, 77, 78, 79, 91, 93, 102, 105, 107, 108, 109, 110, 111, 115, 116, 117, 118, 119, 122, 124, 125, 133, 135, 136, 137
Enlightenment 8, 123, 124
Epicurus 33
Equality ... 95, 98, 99, 100, 105, 111, 112
Equality and Human Rights Commission 95, 98, 99, 105, 111
Establishment 84, 89, 122
Ethnic 97
Europe .... xix, 2, 5, 9, 17, 117, 124
European .. xiv, 10, 17, 18, 19, 28, 32, 64, 95, 102, 104, 112, 115, 118, 119, 122, 124, 126, 128
European Union xiv, 102, 104, 115, 118, 119, 122, 124, 128
Euroscepticism 89

F

Fairbanks, Douglas 27
Fascism 81
Fassbinder, Rainer Werner 2
FBI 23
Forsyth, Bruce 20
Foucault,, Michel 116
Fox News 66
Freud, Sigmund 31
Froude, James Anthony iv

G

Gable, Gerry 61
Gadd, Paul 34
Galileo .... iii, 25
Gay 5, 13, 18
Georgism 101
Germany 17, 19
Gestapo 99
Gielgud, John 88
God .... viii, xviii, 10, 23, 27
Goebbels, Josef 43
Gove, Michael 105
Gramsci, Antonio 116
Griffin,, Nick xix, 51, 67, 69, 81, 83, 86, 96, 98, 104, 106, 107, 108, 111, 114
Guardian 37, 67, 81, 82, 90, 91, 92, 105, 116, 137

H

Hague, William 65, 136
Hain, Peter 93
Hames, Mike 24
Hamza, Abu 70
Hapsburg 119
Hayek, Friedrich August von 101
Hegelian 86
Hindley, Moira .... vii, 7, 8
Hitchcock, Alfred 27
Hitler, Adolf 17, 86, 99, 108, 115, 125
Holocaust 23, 120, 124
Homosexuality .... xvii, 5
House of Lords 100
Howerd, Frankie 31
Hume, David 101
Humour 49
Huxley, Aldous viii
Hyams, Roland 5

I

Ideology 115
Inquisition .... viii, 82
Institute for Jewish Policy Research. 120, 123
Internet ... vi, 32, 33, 41, 93, 97, 120, 121, 122, 123, 135
Irving, David 127
Isherwood, Christopher 18
Islam .... v, xviii, xx, 51, 63, 91

Israel 127
ITV3 31

J

James I 100
James II 100
Jasper, Lee 90
Jesus 9
Jew .... iii, 46, 86, 87, 100, 101, 112, 126, 127
Jokes 45
Jordan 121
Judaism .... xviii, 63
Juries 13, 25
Justice 35, 124, 130

K

Katyn Wood 125
Kersey, John .... xvii, xviii
KGB 99

L

Labour Party 41, 79, 87, 88, 102, 110
Lammy 91
Law 10, 11, 24, 125
Lawrence 2
LBC 49
LBPA 97
Lemon 13
Liberal Party 87, 135
Libertarian ..... xviii, 1, 24, 30, 45, 83, 84, 87, 90, 94, 124, 125, 127, 129, 133
Libertarian Alliance .. xviii, 1, 24, 45, 83, 84, 87, 90, 94, 124, 125, 127, 129
Liberty .... iii, v, 94, 98
Literature .... iv, 25
Lloyd George 85
Locke 101
LONDON .... 3, 4, iv, xvi, 1, 2, 5, 6, 8, 9, 10, 11, 12, 17, 18, 24, 41, 42, 43, 49, 60, 62, 66, 68, 72, 73, 78, 82, 90, 91, 92, 95, 98, 107, 113, 116, 120, 136
Loughborough 7
Loughner 66, 67, 69
Louis 79, 116
Luton Grammar School 30
Lynn vi
Lysenko iii

M

Magna Carta 96
Major, John 1, 29
Mandelson, Peter 47, 99
Marr, Andrew 116
Marx, Karl .... viii, 9, 63, 69
Marxism 93
Marxist-Leninism 9
Mass-Immigration 102, 118
Media 19
Mein Kampf viii
Mill, John Stuart ... ii, iii, v, xv, 101, 110, 117, 118, 134
Milton, John 3, 134
Monocled Mutineer 20
Mountbatten, Lord 50
Murdoch, Rupert 42, 66
Mussolini, Benito 85

N

Napoleon 17
National Assembly Against Racism .. 60, 90
NCROPA 1, 31
Nilsen, Denis 68

O

Obama, Barack 66
Operation Black Vote 95, 96, 97

P

Paedophile Information Exchange xiv
Pasolini, Pier Paolo .... vii, 2
Pasteur, Louis iii
Peel, Robert 53
Phillips, Trevor 135
Police .xii, xiv, 10, 12, 13, 16, 17, 23, 24, 25, 28, 31, 61, 97, 100
Pornography iv, v, 2, 4, 7, 10, 11, 14, 23, 31
Protocols of the Learned Elders of Zion viii
Public Order Act 1986 xvi

Q

Querelle 2

R

Race Relations Act 1976 ....95, 105, 106, 112, 113
Randall and Hopkirk 30
Rechy, John 2
Rees-Mogg, William 21
Reformation 9
Reid, John 99
Renaissance 67, 68
Revolution .... xix, 116
Rite of Spring 92

S

Sainsbury 16
Salò .... vii, 2
Salome 12
Satanic Verses viii
Savile, Jimmy 135, 136
Schauer, Frederick 3
Searchlight 121
Simon Wiesenthal Center 121
Skinner, Denis 42, 43
Snuff Video 22
Soley, Clive 129
Spanner Case 75
Spectator 51
Stalin, Josef 9, 99
Stamp, Terence 116
State .. 3, 4, v, xii, xiv, xv, 19, 21, 43, 74, 95, 99, 100, 105, 106, 109, 124, 127, 130, 133
Sutcliffe, Peter 10
Swinburne, Algernon Charles 8

T

Tame, Chris 54, 78, 83
Tatchell, Peter .... xix, 72
Terrorism 23
Thatcher, Margaret 16, 19, 21, 25, 29, 32, 41, 42, 43, 44, 46, 47, 48, 70
Theatres Act 11
Thief of Baghdad 27
Toleration xix
Tristan und Isolde 92
Trotskyism 86
Tyndal, John 86

U

United Kingdom. 10, 16, 17, 18, 46, 110, 112
United Nations .... xiv, 122
United States 23, 70
Upstairs, Downstairs 30

V

Vidal, Gore 18, 30
Visions of Ecstasy 27
Voltaire, François 9, 75

W

Wadham,, John 98, 99, 113
Waugh, Aubern 51
Webb, Auberon 1, 30, 31
Well of Loneliness 2, 10
Whitehouse, Mary .. 7, 10, 12, 13, 16, 23, 29
Whitelaw, William 32
Wilde, Oscar 12, 18
Williams Report 13, 16, 25
Wogan, Terry 20
Wolfenden, Lord 131
Woolley, Simon 96

144